COAST

RECIPES INSPIRED BY IRELAND'S WILD ATLANTIC COAST

RACHEL ALLEN

HarperCollins*Publishers*

Welcome to COAST, my journey along the rugged, wildly beautiful Atlantic coast of Ireland.

Recently I hit the road and went on a culinary trip from my home county of Cork all the way up to the green, untamed headlands of Donegal. Along the way I visited major coastal villages and towns, meeting local food producers and cooks, sampling their sensational produce, watching them at work and tasting their delicious recipes. It was an inspirational odyssey, and an adventure unlike anything I have ever undertaken before.

Here, I want to share with you all the influences and impressions from my trip: my favourite places to stay off the beaten track, the incredible stories I heard from the fishermen and farmers that I encountered, and the breadth of local produce – from honey and cheeses to gins and whiskeys – that, of course, I just had to sample along the way!

I may be biased, but I believe that Ireland's Atlantic coast has some of the most beautiful scenery in the world, and a wonderfully rich food heritage to match. There were years, even decades, when Ireland was branded a nation of potato and cabbage eaters, but we have overturned that opinion and now stand proud of the fabulous dishes that have been created here for generations, knowing that when it is cooked with a delicate touch, our traditional and contemporary food is hard to beat. Particularly so when it is cooked here in Ireland from our own home-grown produce.

And we have some of the best produce in the world. When it's prepared simply and without unnecessary embellishments, it's absolutely second to none; we have sheep that can roam free, cattle that get to eat perfectly green grass and wild flowers all year round, coastal walks and woodlands scented with the aroma of wild garlic, watercress that is there for the foraging, and seafood that's sweet and delicate because of our bitingly cold fresh waters.

Our distilleries produce not just the fabulous whiskeys for which Ireland is famed, but as you will discover through my journey, fabulously flavoured gins, not to mention the legendary beers our brewers make. Our sheep and cattle provide us with milk for delicious artisan cheeses with traditional flavours, but Ireland is also at the cutting edge of food production, with Mediterranean-style cheeses being produced from buffalo's and goat's milk.

Farmers' markets are thriving all over Ireland, selling produce that is lovingly and patiently cultivated, created and prepared for sale. A stroll through one of these markets is a feast for the senses and the sheer range of delicious home-produced food will astound you.

This journey has reminded me how much I love Ireland, my beautiful Emerald Isle. I adore tasting all of the different foods each corner of the world has to offer, but no matter where I travel across the globe, it is the flavours and aromas of fresh, seasonal, simple Irish cooking that makes me feel most at home.

Coast is filled with stunning photography of the people and places that I visited in my travel, giving you snapshots of the beauty of this wild, natural landscape, and hopefully a sense of my Ireland – a country of traditions and modern practices that sit in harmony, creating a unique approach to food. Of course, I couldn't complete my journey without sharing with you some of the recipes that were inspired by my experiences, so here are a whole host of authentic and simple recipes. From Salmon pâté and Pan-fried fish with watercress butter, to Irish gingerbread and Gin, lemon and milk ice cream, these are simple dishes made with the freshest ingredients – fuss-free and yet packed full of flavour.

Coast is a book from my heart – my Ireland, my food, my passions all rolled into one. I hope you enjoy it as much as I've enjoyed the journey to create it.

I can feel rising excitement about the trip I'm about to embark on from my home at Ballymaloe.

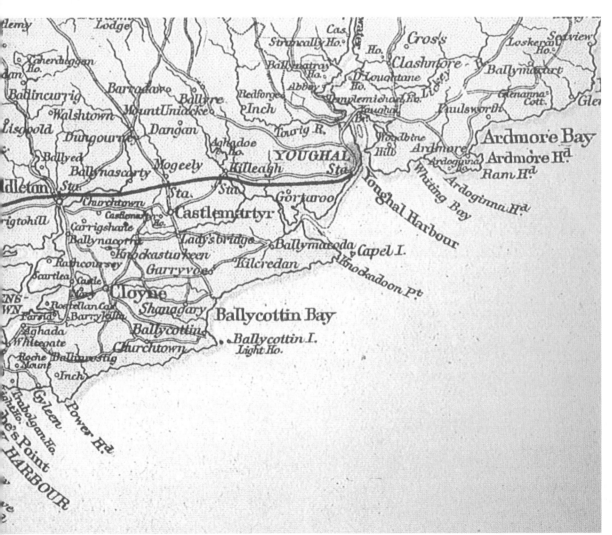

HOME

CO. CORK

HOME

Poring over the map of Ireland that is laid out in front of me, I can feel
rising excitement about the trip I'm about to embark on. I have just twelve
days in which to explore the best of the wild Atlantic coast – from my home
at Ballymaloe right around the latticed western coastline, venturing as far
as Inishowen in County Donegal.

Along the way I know I'll experience some of the breathtaking scenic
highlights of Ireland's countryside, visit some of the country's most historic sites
and meet with inspiring restaurateurs and food producers who will no doubt be
eager to share their food and their passion for cooking with me. This is an area
that revels in its abundant local, seasonal ingredients – from the sea and the land.

But all journeys start with a first step (and no small amount of preparation),
so to get my road legs in order I need to do a little exploring around my own
area first. I've decided on a trip up the gorgeous Blackwater Valley through
County Cork. But before I get going, of course, I need to pack a few provisions!

Close to my home in Midleton there is a great farmers' market that I often visit
on Saturday mornings, where table after table groans with delicious breads, freshly
picked fruit and veg, jewel-like bottles of jams and pickles glinting in the sun.
I love chatting to the stallholders there about what they produce, and how they
produce it – their passion for their products is clear to see and rubs off on me. As
ever, the stalls offer tantalising selections of some of the very best produce from all
over the region. Stumped by the array of delicious foods, I steel myself to choose
just a few treats and finally pick up delicious local cheeses, bread and pickles that
I know will make the perfect picnic. The leftovers make really indulgent cheese
toasts on my Irish onion soup (see page 24), but I buy extra, too, because the array
inspires me to create my Bread, wine and cheese gratin (see page 31).

Drink is as important to Midleton as its food. It is home to the largest
distillery complex in the country, right next to the Old Midleton Distillery
that was established here in the early 17th century. They make seven different
types of whiskey here, from Jameson (the best-selling Irish whiskey in the
world) to Midleton Very Rare, which is always a nice bottle to give as a present.
Of course, that's not one I'd use for cooking with – it's a bit special. I was also
introduced to Yellow Spot from this distillery, which is the 12-year version of
the Green Spot whiskey. It's aged in Malaga barrels and it's one of the nicest
whiskies I've ever tasted … I know what I'll be celebrating the end of the trip
with! I sample a few other whiskies, and when I'm back at home later from my
trip I remember the flavours lingering on my palate and know that I need to create
something to pair with. One of the less expensive whiskies, therefore, becomes the

base to my Quick chocolate mousse (see page 34), adding a lovely warm kick to this delicious pudding.

By now I'm getting peckish and I pop over to the Ballymaloe Cookery School where my brother-in-law Philip has a restaurant (on Saturdays only) called 'Saturday Pizzas' where he cooks the best pizzas in the wood-burning oven. There's always a margarita and a pepperoni pizza on the menu, next to whatever seasonal pizza specials he has on for the day. Most of the produce comes from the farm and one of my absolute favourites is the slow-cooked pork pizza with aioli and kale.

Just south of Ballymaloe is the coastal village of Ballycotton; sitting on the grassy cliffs overlooking the brilliant blue sea stretching out into the distance is one of the most relaxing things to do on a summer's day, and there's also a good chance I'll spot a fishing boat or two on the horizon, bringing in fresh catch for local markets and export, too. Fish makes up a large proportion of the recipes in this book; we are really fortunate where we live that we have access to a large range of delicious fish and seafood fresh from the Atlantic. There is nothing better than eating fish that smells of the sea, having left it only a few hours since. The flavours are truly exceptional.

But linger I can't, so it's back on my travels again. This time I head about 20km to the east of Ballymaloe, to the busy port town of Youghal, known for its two lovely Blue Flag beaches (Claycastle and Front Strand). It is also the mouth of the Blackwater River, a scenic and historic body of water that generally exists beneath the tourist radar. To get my journey going, I board the *Maeve*, a half-decker fishing boat captained by Tony Gallagher and his first mate, a terrier called Pharaoh, for a 90-minute tour of the river. This slow passage meanders 8km upwater, allowing me a sneak peek at the beautiful grand houses and gardens that line the back, and ends at the dramatic ruins of Templemichael Castle.

This is where the boat trip culminates, but I want to go further up the Blackwater Valley, so bidding goodbye to Tony and Pharaoh I get back on land and transfer to my car (which has been magically transported upriver by a loving family member!). Esconced at the wheel, I'm off northward, skirting the eastern bank of the river.

At the bend of the river, with the Blackwater Valley stretching out to the west, I stop in the market town Cappoquin, which nestles between the stunning landscapes of the river and the heather-clad Knockmealdown Mountains. The big attraction here is the striking Georgian Cappoquin House and Gardens, but the town is also a popular spot for anglers, as the river is rich in beautiful fresh salmon and trout. You cannot leave here without dreaming of fish! This town makes me want to cook my recipes for Poached salmon with hollandaise sauce (see page 19) and Poached grey sea mullet with coriander vinaigrette (see page 21). I discover that the local tackle shop, Titelines, will sell me the licence I need if I want to try to catch some fish, but I realise that my dreams of such a catch are unlikely to be fulfilled by me with a rod!

On the edge of the town I discover the Blackwater Distillery, Ireland's first craft whiskey distillery. Although I'm always on the lookout for another new whiskey – whether in the hand or in a recipe! – what's of interest to me here is that they've recently launched their very first gin – Blackwater No. 5, a classic London dry gin that uses local botanicals and the soft Blackwater water. The fresh flavours from my essential sampling later inspire me to use a little of it in my aromatic Gin, lemon and milk ice cream (see page 32).

DETOUR: THE TANNERY, DUNGARVAN

I find myself making a little diversion from my northward route. Although it's a little out of my way, I just have to visit one of my favourite spots in the region – Paul Flynn's Tannery restaurant in the port town of Dungarvan. Housed in a converted leather tannery (hence the name), Paul creates consistently fine dishes using local ingredients such as fresh fish and meats and plenty of fruit, veg and herbs – much of it coming from his own abundant organic gardens. Mouthwatering treats such as ceviche of scallops and fennel and braised rose veal belly with salt-baked carrots and courgettes tempt me to linger, not to mention the chocolate and rosemary pot with olive oil cream and blackcurrant veil. Paul's ever-changing menu based on local seasonal produce has helped earn him a reputation as one of the best chefs in Ireland; his clever combining of ingredients creates something surprising and special, and inspires me to think about new pairings of the ingredients I am sampling on my trip. He also runs a cookery school in a gorgeous town house around the corner where you can stay and learn how to use seasonal ingredients in delicious and innovative ways. Sated and revitalised after a marvellous lunch, I reluctantly tear myself away and head back to Cappoquin to continue on with my journey.

About 6km north of Cappoquin I pass the Mount Melleray Cistercian Abbey. If ever I'm feeling in need of a little quiet contemplation, a trip to this beautiful abbey is always a beneficial experience. As I arrive the afternoon sun bathes the ancient building in a beautiful glow, highlighting it against the rolling Irish countryside, picking it out from the surrounding fields. It is a calming and holy place, and the

two dozen or so Trappist monks that live there are always keen to welcome visitors looking for a little meditative time. They have even laid out a lovely tearoom in the cloisters, too, which serves delicious homemade soups and cakes. The rustic simplicity of the food echoes the lifestyle of the monks and I imagine how pleasant a life it must be to live such a simple life of contemplation and prayer, and to grow and cook with ingredients produced within the abbey walls.

There's no time for tea today, though. I make my way westward through Lismore, where its magnificent castle provides the perfect excuse to stop and stretch my legs. I have a nice amble through the ornate formal gardens, beautifully clipped and perfectly placed under the medieval stone walls of the castle. There is no time to venture further into the remainder of the eight acres of gardens that are bursting into bloom, but of course I had to stroll along the famous, elegant yew walk – thought to be the spot on which Edmund Spenser wrote *The Faerie Queene* in 1590. On Sundays, Castle Avenue hosts a superb farmers' market in the castle grounds, populated by producers from all over the region selling their wares – it's a proper gourmet treat. The stalls offer up a beautiful array of local fresh fish, vegetables and fruit, as well as beautiful breads and home-baked pies. Bring a rug, settle down beneath the castle walls or on the banks of the river with your bounty and you have everything you need for the perfect picnic!

Refreshed by my scenic stroll, it's onwards to Ballyduff, where another opportunity for salmon fishing presents itself. The village is perfectly positioned so that you can fish while taking in the glorious views of the river and woodlands beyond. The Ballyduff Bridge is the prime place – a fishing beat that's almost a mile long, has a wide variety of water and is especially good for fly fishing. Local experts such as Ballyduff Bridge Salmon Fishery and ghillies Len Tomlinson and Connie Corcoran offer provide expert tuition and advice on how best to catch salmon for those new to the sport. I think I am one who would need their help!

As the sun begins to set I reach my final destination for my first day on this journey. Heading south-west from Ballyduff I reach Ballyvolane House, a gracious Georgian mansion expertly run by Justin and Jenny Green. As I approach the house, immediately I feel relaxed after my day of driving. Everything about this place is idyllic, from the beautifully finished rooms to the wonderful gardens and – the food. This really is a foodie paradise: everything that appears on plates in the restaurant is sourced from the estate and local artisan producers – rare-breed pigs are reared on site, beef and lamb come from nearby Lismore, fish fresh from Cork and home-produced artisan cheeses from Cork, Waterford and Tipperary. The vegetables and fruit are all freshly picked from Ballyvolane's walled garden, straight from plot to plate. The four-course menu for dinner sends me to bed satisfied and content, having experienced a culinary tour of Cork and its environs in just one meal.

POACHED SALMON WITH HOLLANDAISE SAUCE

Whether wild salmon is from the sea or the river, when it's in season I think this is the best way to serve it. Add a few boiled new potatoes and delicious summer vegetables such as peas, broad beans or samphire, or if still in season, asparagus or sea kale, and you have the quintessential summer main course.

Serves 4 as a main course

salt
18–20cm (7–8in) piece of salmon, still on the bone, cut from a whole fish that has been gutted and descaled (ask your fishmonger to do this if necessary)

FOR THE HOLLANDAISE SAUCE
1 egg yolk
60g (2½oz) butter
a little squeeze of lemon juice

Choose a saucepan, or oval casserole, that will just fit the fish, as snugly as possible. If you choose a saucepan much larger than the piece of fish a lot of the flavour and goodness from the salmon will go into the water. Take the salmon out of the pot and set aside.

Place water into the pan to fill it by half or two-thirds. Measure the water and add 1 tablespoon of salt for every 1.2 litres (2 pints) water. Place the pan on a high heat and bring to the boil. Carefully place the salmon in the pan, making sure it's covered with water, and bring back up to the boil. Turn the heat down, cover with a lid and gently simmer for 20 minutes. Remove from the heat and leave the salmon to stand in the cooking liquid, with the lid still on, for 5 minutes – the fish will continue to cook.

Now make the hollandaise sauce. Put the egg yolk in a bowl big enough to whisk in. Bring the butter to a foaming boil in a pan, then pour it slowly, in a thin stream, over the egg yolk, whisking all the time. Stir in a few drops of lemon juice, then set aside somewhere warm (or keep warm as for Pickled ginger beurre blanc on page 104).

Carefully remove the salmon from the water, then remove the skin (and, if you wish, any brown flesh by scraping gently with a small, sharp knife). Run a knife or fish slice carefully down along the bone to release the flesh away from the bone on either side, then lift the flesh off, giving four portions in total.

Serve immediately with the hollandaise sauce.

POACHED GREY SEA MULLET WITH CORIANDER VINAIGRETTE

A nice big chunk of fish on the bone, at least 900g (2lb) in weight, is needed for this dish. Don't cook a fish steak or cutlet like this, as you'll lose too much flavour from the flesh. A 2kg (4lb 4oz) mullet will feed 6–8 people very well. You need only water, salt and a saucepan or a fish kettle, to cook the fish.

Serves 4–8 as a main course, depending on size of fish

salt
1 whole mullet, 1–2kg (2lb 2oz–4lb 4oz) in weight, gutted, or a piece of fish,
    about 900g (2lb), cut through the bone (a whole mullet with the head will
    obviously weigh less once the head is removed after cooking)

FOR THE CORIANDER VINAIGRETTE
60ml (2½fl oz) extra virgin olive oil
20ml (¾fl oz) sherry vinegar
1 generous tbsp chopped coriander
2 tsp coriander seeds, toasted and ground (see page 149)
1 generous tbsp chopped spring onions
salt and freshly ground black pepper

Half-fill a large saucepan, oval casserole or fish kettle with measured water and add 1 tablespoon salt to each 1.2 litres (2 pints) water. Add the fish and bring to the boil, then turn down the heat, cover the pan and simmer (do not boil vigorously or the fish will overcook around the edges) for 20 minutes. Turn off the heat and leave the fish to sit in the water for at least 5 minutes, or up to 20 minutes.

Meanwhile, mix all the ingredients together for the coriander vinaigrette and season to taste with salt and pepper.

To serve, carefully lift the fish out of the water and place on a warm plate. Peel off the skin, then lift portions of the fish away from the bones. When you've lifted all the meat from one side, turn it over and do the same on the other side.

Serve the coriander vinaigrette spooned over the warm fish.

RACHEL'S TIP
This method also works well for cooking salmon, trout or bass, whole or in a large piece.

CEVICHE

I always remember my first taste of ceviche. It was back in 1990 when I was doing the cookery course at Ballymaloe. Susie Noriega, one of our teachers, who is Peruvian, taught us how to make it. I immediately adored this incredibly fresh-tasting Latin American starter of raw fish simply marinated in citrus juice, with some chillies, tomatoes and peppers thrown in for good measure.

Fast forward twenty-odd years and ceviche has become almost commonplace on this side of the world, with it appearing on myriad restaurant menus and even whole restaurants serving nothing but the dish itself.

I love mixing and matching the different fruit and vegetables in a ceviche, from avocado and sweetcorn to watermelon with cucumber. This is raw food at its best.

Serves 4 as a starter

300g (11oz) very fresh filleted fish (round or flat fish will work), very thinly
    sliced
75ml (3fl oz) lime juice
2 tbsp extra virgin olive oil
1 tsp cumin seeds, toasted and ground (see page 149)
2 pinches of salt
1 ripe avocado, halved, stone removed, peeled and flesh chopped into 1cm (½in) dice
100g (3½oz) fresh tomatoes, chopped into 1cm (½in) dice
1 tbsp finely chopped red onion
2 tbsp chopped coriander

Place the fish in a bowl, add the lime juice, olive oil, cumin and salt and leave to sit for 1 hour.

When ready to serve, mix all the remaining ingredients together and combine with the fish, then serve.

IRISH ONION SOUP WITH BLUE CHEESE TOASTS

Just like a French onion soup, but because we have such great cream in Ireland I thought, why not add some in? I love the salty tang that you get from blue cheese, but of course feel free to use any other cheese.

Serves 4 as a starter

25g (1oz) butter
600g (1lb 6oz) onions, peeled and cut into 5mm (¼in) thick slices
salt and freshly ground black pepper
1 litre (1¾ pints) chicken or beef stock
150ml (5fl oz) double or regular cream

FOR THE BLUE CHEESE TOASTS
8 x 1cm (½in) thick slices of baguette, white yeast bread or sourdough
75g (3oz) blue cheese, crumbled

Melt the butter in a saucepan large enough to take the onions. Add the onions, season with salt and pepper and stir. Turn the heat down to medium–low and cook for 1¼–1½ hours until the onions are very deep golden brown. You'll need to stir the onions and scrape the bottom of the saucepan every few minutes while cooking.

When the onions have caramelised, add the stock and bring to the boil, then turn the heat down and simmer for 15 minutes. Add the cream, bring to a simmer and season to taste again with salt and pepper, then take off the heat.

When ready to serve, preheat the grill, then toast the bread on both sides and cut into smaller pieces, about 4cm (1½in). Pour the hot soup into heatproof bowls and top with the toasted bread. Crumble the blue cheese over the top, place the bowls under the hot grill and cook for 1–2 minutes until bubbling.

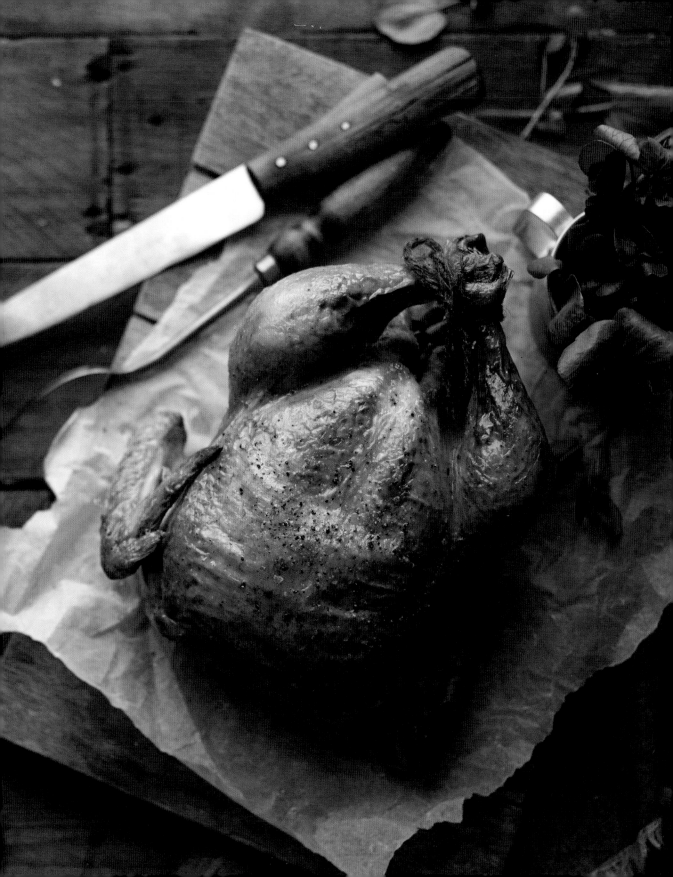

CHICKEN BAKED WITH BUTTER AND WATERCRESS

My husband's grandmother, Myrtle Allen, has been cooking turkey like this for over fifty years at Ballymaloe. You end up with a wonderfully moist and succulent bird that is full of flavour and, of course, the accompanying sauce will just adore some creamy mashed potatoes on the side.

Serves 4-6 as a main course

a few sprigs of watercress
1 whole chicken, giblets and wing tips removed
salt and freshly ground black pepper
25g (1oz) butter
250g (9oz) onion, peeled and chopped
2 cloves of garlic, peeled and crushed or finely grated

FOR THE SAUCE
15g (½oz) butter
75g (3oz) watercress, stalks discarded and leaves chopped
1 small clove of garlic, peeled and crushed or finely grated
125ml (4½fl oz) double or regular cream

Preheat the oven to 180°C (350°F), Gas mark 4.

Place a flameproof casserole or ovenproof saucepan (in which the chicken will fit) on a medium–high heat and allow to get hot.

Place the whole watercress sprigs in the chicken carcass with some salt and pepper. Spread a little of the butter over the breast of the chicken and season with salt and pepper.

Place the chicken, breast side down, in the preheated casserole or pan and brown the chicken breast on both sides, then remove it from the pan. Wipe out the pan with kitchen paper if there's any burnt butter in it.

Add the remaining butter (though not the butter for the sauce) to the pan and let it melt. Add the onion and garlic and season with salt and pepper. Turn the heat down to low, cover the onion with a butter wrapper, some baking parchment or greaseproof paper and the lid. Sweat the onions for about 6 minutes, until softened.

Discard the wrapper or paper, place the chicken on top of the onion, breast side up, cover with the lid and cook in the oven for 1½–2 hours, depending on the size of the chicken. When the chicken is cooked a leg will feel loose in the carcass and there should be no trace of pink between the leg and the breast when you insert the tip of a knife.

Transfer the chicken to a carving dish to rest. Set a sieve over a small heatproof bowl, then tip the juices and onion from the pan into the sieve and push through. Allow the juices to stand for 2 minutes, then skim off any fat and discard.

Put the pan back on a medium heat, add the 15g (½oz) butter for the sauce and, when melted, add the chopped watercress and garlic. Stir over the heat for 1 minute or until the watercress softens, then add the degreased juices from the chicken (and any from the carving dish) and the cream. Bring to the boil, then season to taste with salt and pepper.

Serve the sauce poured over the carved chicken, along with some delicious creamy mashed potatoes and buttered cabbage.

BREAD, WINE AND CHEESE GRATIN

This delicious homely gratin is definitely more than the sum of its parts. Stale bread, leftover cheese and a slosh of wine – just perfect for a cold, blustery evening.

Serves 4 as a brunch, main course or supper

1 tsp butter or extra virgin olive oil
150g (5oz) bacon lardons
150g (5oz) mixed wild mushrooms or plain button or flat mushrooms, sliced
salt and freshly ground black pepper
100g (3½oz) Cheddar cheese, grated
3 tsp Dijon mustard
½ loaf (about 150g/5oz) of white yeast or sourdough bread (a day or two old is perfect)
75ml (3fl oz) white wine (using whatever you have leftover is fine)
450g (1lb) farmhouse cheese (I love using a semi-soft cheese such as Gubbeen, Mileens, Durras or a mixture)
1 tsp chopped thyme leaves

Preheat the oven to 220°C (425°F), Gas mark 7.

Place a frying pan on a high heat and add the butter or olive oil. Add the lardons and cook for 6–8 minutes until golden. Lift the bacon out, leaving any fat or oil in the pan, and set aside. Tip the mushrooms into the pan and season with salt and pepper. Cook for about 5 minutes until soft and golden, then set aside.

Mix the Cheddar with the mustard and spread over the bottom of a 2 litre (3½ pint) gratin dish. Break the bread into big chunks, about 4cm (1½in) in size, and spread over the cheese in the dish. Drizzle the wine over the top, then cook in the oven for 10–15 minutes until slightly golden around the edges.

Take out of the oven and arrange the mushrooms over the bread. Cut the farmhouse cheese, with all its rind, into wedges, about 2cm (¾in) wide at its widest, and arrange over the mushrooms, then scatter with the thyme. The dish can be prepared ahead to this point. Put back into the oven and cook again for a further 10–15 minutes until golden and bubbling. Serve.

GIN, LEMON AND MILK ICE CREAM

Who knew gin with lemon and milk could be so good? This adult ice cream is just divine enjoyed on its own, or with berries on the side.

Serves 4

1 egg, separated
250ml (9fl oz) milk
grated zest and juice of ½ lemon
140g (4¾oz) caster sugar
75ml (3fl oz) gin

Cones to serve

In a bowl, whisk together the egg yolk with the milk, lemon zest and juice, sugar and gin.

In a clean dry bowl, whisk the egg white to a stiff peak and stir into the milk mixture, then use the whisk briefly to combine the two mixtures.

Freeze in a sorbetière, or in a bowl in the freezer, taking it out halfway through to give it a very good whisk to break up the ice crystals.

Serve in a cone or bowl.

QUICK CHOCOLATE MOUSSE

This is, without doubt, my go-to dessert to whip up in five minutes. Delicious served with simply a few raspberries sitting on top, or softly whipped cream and a sweet sticky toffee sauce.

Serves 4

120g (4¼oz) dark chocolate, chopped or in chips
120ml (4fl oz) double or regular cream
2 eggs
finely grated zest of 1 small orange (optional)
1–2 tbsp Irish whiskey (optional)

Put the chocolate in a heatproof bowl. In a pan on a high heat, bring the cream to the boil, then pour it over the chocolate and stir to melt.

Separate the eggs and beat the egg yolks into the melted chocolate. You can add the orange zest or whiskey with the egg yolks, if you wish.

In a separate, clean, grease-free bowl, whisk the egg whites until just holding a stiff peak, then carefully fold them into the chocolate.

Spoon into individual bowls or glasses and place in the fridge for at least 1½ hours to set.

Cork is a great city for wandering around in. It is packed onto an island surrounded by the River Lee, and the compact city centre is a treasure trove of 17ᵗʰ-century alleys, broad streets, historic buildings and contemporary architecture.

CORK CITY

CO. CORK

CORK CITY

Having explored the countryside around me, it's time to head into the city; Cork City, that is, the 'real capital of Ireland' (as Corkonians like to say!).

Any time I'm up in the city I invariably make a beeline for the Crawford Municipal Art Gallery. It's not just about the culture – although with a permanent collection that runs the gamut from the 17th century to today, you can get lost in the gallery. You can take in works by Sir John Lavery, Jack B. Yeats and Nathaniel Hone, beautiful stained-glass windows by Harry Clarke, amble through a sculpture gallery populated by snow-white plaster casts (made by Canova in 1816 from originals in the Vatican and then gifted by the Pope to George IV) and finish up in my favourite room, devoted to women artists from 1886 to 1978, which includes works by Irish artists Mainie Jellet and Evie Hone. Finally, the gentle waft of mouthwatering aromas from the café calls an end to my cultural tour; I feel I have earned a visit. Whenever I am here I always make a point of stopping for a bite of lunch or coffee and cake – today I'm feeling really peckish and it's still morning, so the wonderful Eggs Benedict it is for me! Or, if I'm short of time, then it's the best flat white in town I'm after and I head to the gorgeously cosy Café Idaho.

Cork is a great city for wandering around in. It is packed onto an island surrounded by the River Lee, and the compact city centre is a treasure trove of 17th-century alleys, broad streets, historic buildings and contemporary architecture that makes for a pleasant day's exploring.

Inevitably I find myself migrating towards the produce-lined corridors of the English Market, probably the best-known covered market in the country and to my mind a rival to any market you'll find anywhere in Europe. Beneath its high, vaulted Victorian ceilings are scores of vendors selling some of the best local produce available. It is a bustling blend of stalls and produce – I love the eclectic mix of traditional old-school butchers that have been trading down through the generations at the market alongside the newer young artisan producers from the area. The sounds and smells of the busy market lure you in, and you could easily get lost inside. When I'm there, I always make sure to check out the fabulous selection of charcuterie and cheeses at On the Pig's Back, the beautiful fresh fish at Kay O'Connell's stall, which is something of a Cork institution, or that of Ballycotton Seafood. I inhale the aromas, and after my visit it is the memory of this foodie paradise that inspires me to cook Smoked haddock and cockle soup (see page 47) and Bacon with parsley sauce (see page 54). The cuts of meat laid out by Michael Bresnan, whose grandfather Michael first began trading meat in the market in 1898, and the lush colours of the fresh vegetables spilling out of

boxes around the market inspire my delicious seasonal dish, Pork with cream and watercress (see page 57).

The English Market is the perfect place to get a takeaway lunch – among the mêlée are stalls serving up delicious sandwiches and soups, homemade pies, quiches and slices of pizza. The clamour of hungry visitors ordering their lunch rings through the building, and tells you that you are in for a treat. On sunny days I take my lunch and eat it in nearby Bishop Lucey Park, a large and very welcome green space in a busy, urban setting, where you can watch the world go by as you munch, savouring every flavour in a quiet moment out of a busy day. But if it's something more formal you are after, you're spoilt for choice. There are so many excellent options in town for all kinds of moods – from cheap and cheerful to a full-on gourmet dining experience. The Farmgate Café is just upstairs from the market, so if I felt like a fresh, vibrant flavoursome soup, once I've shopped for ingredients to make my Raw beetroot soup (see page 61), that's where I go – for inspiration, of course!

My favourite places include dinner at Isaacs on McCurtain St, The Club Brasserie on Lapp's Quay, Jacques or Les Gourmandises – which is elegant and wonderfully French. Even the city's pubs have got in on the act: Arthur Mayne's is a lovely pub in an old pharmacy, and has a fine selection of wines to accompany really good tapas and Italian-style nibbles. My Calamari with roast red pepper aioli (see page 48) is inspired by great tapas classics, as is my Squid, tuna and fennel stew with chorizo (see page 52). If I'm in town for Sunday brunch, Goldbergs on Victoria Road, just off Albert Quay, is a terrific spot, serving up spicy scrambled eggs on local sourdough, nutritious homemade smoothies, warm, freshly baked scones or delicious soups, salads and sandwiches. The vast breakfast menu here made me mull over brunch recipes, and once home in my kitchen I came up with my Smoked haddock florentine (see page 44), a substantial brunch dish using great ingredients from local seasonal suppliers.

When I've finished browsing the myriad mouthwatering stalls, it's lunchtime and the moment when I must make a decision about where I'm going to eat. I could go to Zamora for a hearty salad, stew or soup and a nice glass of house cava, but instead I opt for a bit of pub grub in the Long Valley Bar, where I order a corned beef sandwich and wash it down with a glass of Beamish – it doesn't get any more traditional than that!

After lunch I pay a visit to the Rising Sons Brewery, Cork's newest microbrewery. It produces 50 kegs of chemical- and additive-free beer that are available in any of the city's heritage pubs, including the delicious Mi Daza, Handsum IPA and Sunbeam Pilsner. My visit to this brewery inspired my Beer bread with caramelised onions and blue cheese (see

page 64). Beer is definitely not just for drinking!

Hunger sated, it's time to head out of the city centre. At the south-wesern edge of the city is Mahon Point, which, every Thursday, has my favourite farmers' market of all. Its great selection of stalls and super-quality produce have people coming in their droves to shop, eat or just drink fab coffee. My next stop is about 11km south of here, just outside the village of Carrigaline. Ann and Pat O'Farrell's farm produces three kinds of cheese – an all-natural, semi-soft cheese; a garlic- and herb-flavoured cheese; and a maple-smoked cheese, all of which are handmade with milk from the Frieisian cows that graze the rolling fields around the farm.

With so many thoughts of fine food in my head, I finally depart the city itself and begin my journey westward along the Wild Atlantic coast. I've spent so much time in Cork City that it's late afternoon by the time I make it to my first stop – which is only 20km away!

Kinsale is a lovely town teaming with sailing boats bobbing up and down on the gentle waters of the marina and lots of pretty little shops lining the streets around the harbour. It's also the gateway to West Cork, where so many of the county's best producers ply their glorious trade. One of the most famous spots in town is probably Martin and Marie Shanahan's Fishy Fishy, which has won plenty of kudos for its wonderful dishes made with locally caught seafood, from wok-fried clams to beautifully battered haddock with homemade fries and their lovely lobster Thermidor.

Tonight, though, I'm heading into the Black Pig Wine Bar, which has a delicious selection of tapas and cheese boards to go with its enormous wine list – there are about 80 wines by the bottle and 40 available by the glass. It's been a long day, but this is the ideal way to end it, over some locally cured cheese and home-cured carpaccio, washed down with a nice glass of Alta Vista Malbec – just perfect!

I crawl into my bed at the elegant Perryville House, and sleep until morning and my next gourmet day begins again, with home-baked bread and fresh products from local slow food growers.

SMOKED HADDOCK FLORENTINE

I always find it hard to resist Eggs Florentine when I see them on a menu, and this recipe is just as special, with the addition of smoked haddock and dark leafy cavolo nero. This treat will keep you going all day.

Serves 2

10g (scant ½oz) butter, plus extra for the toast
2 x 100g (3½oz) pieces smoked haddock (ask for undyed)
2 slices of bread, toasted (I love to use a sourdough for this)
2 lovely fresh free-range eggs
1 x quantity of hollandaise sauce (see page 19)
twist of black pepper, to serve

FOR THE CAVOLO NERO
75g (3oz) cavolo nero, weighed after the stalks have been removed, washed, no need
    to chop (or you can use curly kale or spinach)
good pinch of salt
10g (scant ½oz) butter

Bring 500ml (18fl oz) water to a rolling boil in a saucepan. Add a pinch of salt, then the cavolo nero and boil, uncovered, for 2–3 minutes until tender (spinach will cook faster). Drain well, squeezing out the liquid, then return to the pan with the butter. Remove from the heat and set aside.

Bring a pan of water to the boil for poaching the eggs.

Heat the butter and 1 tablespoon of water in a small pan. When the butter is melted and foaming, add the fish, cover with a lid and turn the heat down to low. Cook for a few minutes until the fish is cooked in the centre.

Put the eggs into the simmering water (do not boil). Warm the cavolo nero and pour in any juices from the fish pan. Butter the toast, add a nest of cavolo nero, place the fish on it and top with a poached egg. Spoon the hollandaise sauce over, twist over some black pepper and serve at once.

SMOKED HADDOCK AND COCKLE SOUP

A deliciously rich and smooth smoked haddock and potato soup, with sweet salty cockles sitting on top.

Serves 4 as a starter

20–30 cockles in their shells, well washed and scrubbed – discard any that are not
    tightly shut or don't close when tapped
50ml (2fl oz) white wine
25g (1oz) butter
125g (4½oz) chopped onions
125g (4½oz) chopped trimmed fennel bulb (reserve any fennel fronds from the top)
¼ tsp salt
good twist of black pepper
175g (6oz) peeled, chopped potato
125g (4½oz) smoked haddock, trimmed, boned and cut into 1cm (½in) dice
450ml (16fl oz) fish or light chicken stock
100ml (3½fl oz) double or regular cream

Put the cockles and wine in a saucepan and cover with a lid. Put on a high heat and steam until the cockles open. This will take only a few minutes but they will need an occasional stir. When they are all open, transfer to a heatproof bowl with any juices and set aside for later. Discard any cockles that remain closed.

Put the butter into the same saucepan, then add the onion and fennel and season with the salt and pepper. Cover and cook on a low heat for 5 minutes. Add the potato, put the lid back on and cook for 10 minutes, stirring every so often and being careful not to brown the vegetables. Add the smoked haddock and stock and bring to the boil, then turn the heat down and simmer until the potatoes are totally soft.

Transfer to a blender and whiz for a few minutes. Clean out the pan and return the blended soup to it through a sieve. Add the cream and reheat, but do not boil.

Divide the cockles among four hot bowls. Pour the soup evenly over the cockles and serve with the snipped fennel fronds on top.

CALAMARI WITH ROAST RED PEPPER AIOLI

I have always adored squid in any shape or form, and none less so than this crispy fried version with the delicious and garlicky roasted red pepper aioli , which by the way would be great with a steak, lamb chops or battered and fried fish too.

Serves 4–6

FOR THE RED PEPPER AIOLI
2 egg yolks
1 clove of garlic, peeled and crushed or
    finely grated
2 tsp sherry vinegar
½ tsp smoked paprika
1 tsp Dijon mustard
200ml (7fl oz) sunflower oil
25ml (1fl oz) olive oil
1 red pepper, roasted, peeled, deseeded
    and finely chopped
2 tbsp chopped coriander
1 tsp tomato purée
juice of ½ lime
salt and freshly ground black pepper

FOR THE CALAMARI
sunflower oil for deep-frying
150g (5oz) plain flour
50g (2oz) sesame seeds
1 tsp curry powder (optional)
1 tsp salt
1 tsp freshly ground black pepper
600g (1lb 6oz) prepared squid tubes
    (head and intestines discarded), sliced
    1cm (¾in) thick, soaked in milk for at
    least 5 minutes (use the tentacles and
    wings, cut into strips, too if you
    have them)

First roast the pepper. Using your hands, rub the skin with olive oil and place on a tray in an oven preheated to 230°C. Cook for 35-40 minutes until the skin is blackened in patches and the flesh is soft inside (the pepper should be starting to collapse).

Remove from the oven and place in a bowl, cover with cling film and leave for 10 minutes to steam (this will make the skins easier to remove). Next peel the peppers, discarding the skin and seeds.

To make the aioli, put the egg yolks, garlic, vinegar, paprika and mustard in a bowl and whisk to combine. Place the two oils in a jug and pour very slowly into the egg yolk mixture in a thin steady stream, whisking all the time. It will thicken as it emulsifies. Add all the remaining aioli ingredients and season to taste with salt and pepper.

Heat some sunflower oil in a deep-fryer. Mix all the dry ingredients in a large bowl, then toss in the squid and stir to coat in the flour. Shake off the excess flour, then deep-fry, in batches if necessary.

Drain on kitchen paper and serve with the aioli.

SQUID, TUNA AND FENNEL STEW WITH CHORIZO

A big chunky and rustic stew that reminds me of something similar that I ate in San Sebastián many years ago. The fennel aioli, with its intensely garlicky flavour and rich velvety texture, delivers an extra dimension.

Serves 6 as a main course

2 tbsp extra virgin olive oil

2 onions, peeled and finely sliced

2 cloves of garlic, peeled and crushed or finely grated

salt and freshly ground black pepper

800g (1¾lb) fresh tomatoes, peeled and chopped, or 2 x 400g tins of chopped tomatoes

150g (5oz) chorizo, peeled if cured (soft, fresh chorizo doesn't need peeling) and halved lengthways, then cut into 5mm (¼in) thick slices

450g (1lb) peeled potatoes, cut into 2cm (¾in) dice

2 tsp sugar

450g (1lb) (about 4 squid) prepared squid tubes (weighed after head and intestines discarded), cut into rings about 5mm (¼in) thick (use the tentacles and wings too if you have them)

400g (14oz) fresh tuna, filleted and skinned, cut into 2 x 3cm (¾ x 1¼in) chunks

3 tsp ground fennel seeds (don't toast before grinding)

2 tbsp lemon juice

FOR THE FENNEL AIOLI (MAKES 300ML/11FL OZ)

2 egg yolks

1 large clove of garlic, peeled and crushed or finely grated

1 tbsp lemon juice

1 tsp Dijon mustard

pinch of salt

100ml (3½fl oz) sunflower oil

100ml (3½fl oz) extra virgin olive oil

2 tsp ground fennel seeds (don't toast before grinding)

2 tbsp chopped fennel

To make the fennel aioli, put all the ingredients except the oils and fennel (ground and fresh) into a bowl and whisk to combine. Add the olive oil in a very slow trickle, whisking constantly. When all the oil is added you should have a soft, thick consistency. Mix in the ground and fresh fennel and season to taste.

To make the stew, place a large pan on a medium heat, add the olive oil, then the onions and garlic. Season with salt and pepper, then stir, turn the heat down slightly, cover and cook for 8–10 minutes until the onions are soft.

Add the tomatoes, chorizo, potatoes, sugar, squid, salt and pepper and 150ml (5fl oz) water. Stir and bring to a gentle simmer, then turn the heat down to low, cover and cook for 20 minutes or until the potatoes are tender.

Add the tuna and cook for a further 4–5 minutes until cooked, then add the ground fennel seeds and the lemon juice and season to taste with salt and pepper.

Serve hot with a generous blob of aioli over each serving.

BACON WITH PARSLEY SAUCE

Bacon with parsley sauce is an institution in Ireland. It can be really quite plain and dare I say boring, or it can be fabulous. Freshly cooked bacon with a hint of saltiness served with a creamy parsley sauce and delicious green cabbage tossed in butter on the hob till just tender – this is Irish food at its best.

Serves 6 as a main course

900g (2lb) loin or collar of bacon,
   off the bone

FOR THE PARSLEY SAUCE
500ml (18fl oz) milk
½ carrot, sliced
½ onion, peeled and sliced
1 sprig of fresh parsley

1 sprig of fresh thyme
3 peppercorns
25g (1oz) soft butter
25g (1oz) plain flour
1–2 tsp Dijon mustard
25g (1oz) parsley leaves, finely chopped
salt and freshly ground black pepper

Place the bacon in a large saucepan, cover with cold water and bring slowly to the boil. If lots of salty froth floats on the surface when the water boils and the water tastes very salty, drain the pan and refill with fresh cold water and boil again. You want to remove excess salt, but how much depends on how salty the bacon is.

Once the water is boiling, turn the heat down, cover the pan with a lid and simmer for about 40 minutes (45 minutes per 1kg/2lb 2oz), occasionally skimming any sediment that rises to the surface. Once the bacon is cooked (a skewer inserted in the middle should come out easily), remove from the pan, cover with scrunched up baking parchment, and a clean tea towel or an upturned bowl and leave to rest.

While the bacon is cooking, prepare the parsley sauce. Pour the milk into a saucepan and add the carrot, onion, parsley, thyme and peppercorns. Bring to the boil, then turn the heat down and simmer for 1–2 minutes. Remove from the heat and leave to infuse for about 10 minutes.

Melt the butter over a medium heat, add the flour and cook for one minute. Strain the milk over the butter and flour mixture and allow to boil, whisking all the time, until thickened, then stir in the mustard and parsley and season to taste. Take off the heat, cover and keep warm in the pan.

Remove the rind from the bacon and slice into thick pieces. Serve with buttered cabbage and the parsley sauce. This would also be delicious with mashed potato or boiled or baked potatoes.

PORK WITH CREAM AND WATERCRESS

The health benefits of watercress have been well known since ancient times and this simple and quick pork dish is a great way to cook the peppery powerhouse leafy green.

Serves 4–6 as a main course

25g (1oz) butter
1 large clove of garlic, peeled and crushed or finely grated
1 bunch of spring onions (about 100g/3½oz), sliced 5mm (¼in) thick
salt and freshly ground black pepper
500g (1lb 2oz) pork fillet (about 1 pork fillet), trimmed, sliced in half
    horizontally and cut into 0.5–1cm (¼–½in) thick slices
175ml (6fl oz) double or regular cream
50g (2oz) watercress, leaves and some stalks, chopped
½ tsp Dijon mustard

Place a frying pan or sauté pan on a medium heat and add the butter. When the butter melts and foams, tip in the garlic and spring onions and season with salt and pepper. Cook for about 2 minutes until almost softened.

Add the pork slices and cook on a high heat for a minute or two on either side. Add the cream, bring to the boil and allow to bubble for 1–2 minutes until the pork is cooked.

Add the watercress and mustard, stir to mix and season to taste. Add 2–3 tablespoons of water if the sauce is too thick. Serve with green vegetables and mashed potatoes.

RAW BEETROOT, FETA AND AVOCADO SALAD WITH TOASTED ALMONDS AND BALSAMIC DRESSING

This is the kind of salad that I return to time and time again. Raw slivers of earthy beetroot combined with salty crumbly feta cheese and soft rich avocado slices, topped with crunchy toasted almonds – oh-so-delicious and nutritious.

Serves 4–6 as a starter

30g (1¼oz) whole almonds, cut lengthways into three slices
180g (generous 6oz) raw beetroot, peeled and sliced on a mandoline or a
    vegetable peeler 1–2mm (½–¾in) thick
1 large ripe avocado, halved, stone removed, peeled and flesh cut into about
    18 slices
30g (1¼oz) watercress, separated into little sprigs
30g (1¼oz) red onion, peeled and sliced on a mandoline or vegetable peeler
    1–2mm (½–¾in) thick
90g (generous 3¼oz) feta cheese, crumbled
few pinches of sea salt flakes

FOR THE BALSAMIC DRESSING
1 tbsp balsamic vinegar
2 tbsp extra virgin olive oil (the best you have)
pinch of fine salt
twist of black pepper

Preheat the oven to 200°C (400°F), Gas mark 6.

Combine all the ingredients for the balsamic dressing and set aside.

Put the almonds on a baking tray and cook in the oven for 3 minutes until golden under the skins. (You can also do this in a frying pan on a medium–high heat.) Set aside.

Arrange the salad ingredients evenly on the plates: a layer of beetroot, about 3 slices of avocado, sprigs of watercress, red onion slices, crumbled feta, a pinch of sea salt flakes and a scattering of toasted almonds.

Drizzle each plate with a generous 1–1½ teaspoons of dressing and serve immediately.

RAW BEETROOT SOUP WITH DILL AND HONEY YOGHURT

This is fast food at its best and intensely flavoursome – earthy beetroot whizzed up with juicy apples, nutty cumin and sweet honey, then topped with a dill and honey yoghurt. You'll have a Samurai spring in your step after a bowl of this!

Serves 4 as a starter

200g (7oz) natural yoghurt
160g (5½oz) peeled, cored and chopped apple
160g (5½oz) peeled raw beetroot, chopped (young tender beetroot is best)
½ clove of garlic
1 tsp toasted and ground cumin seeds (see page 149)
good pinch of salt
good twist of black pepper
1 tbsp cider vinegar
1 tsp honey
walnut oil or extra virgin olive oil, to serve

FOR THE DILL AND HONEY YOGHURT
1 tsp honey
3 tsp chopped dill
50g (2oz) natural yoghurt

Mix all the ingredients for the dill and honey yoghurt together and chill until needed.

Put the yoghurt and apple into a blender with 100ml (3½fl oz) water. First give it a quick blitz, then add all the remaining ingredients except the oil and whiz for a good length of time until as smooth as possible. Pour through a sieve, then chill before serving.

To serve, pour the soup into bowls. Blob on some of the dill and honey yoghurt, then drizzle with walnut or extra virgin olive oil.

BEER BREAD WITH CARAMELISED ONIONS AND BLUE CHEESE

This is a big, gutsy, manly bread if ever there was one. To get the best flavour, make sure to cook the onions nice and slowly until deep golden brown.

Makes 2 loaves

15g (½oz) fresh yeast or 7g dried yeast
15g (½oz) caster sugar
1 x 330ml bottle of red beer or ale, such as 8 Degrees Sunburnt Irish Red or
    Franciscan Well Rebel Red
500g (1lb 2oz) strong white flour, plus extra for dusting
1 tsp salt
550g (1¼lb) onions, peeled and sliced
2 tbsp extra virgin olive oil
2 tbsp Dijon mustard
100g (3½oz) grated cheese, such as Cheddar
75g (3oz) crumbled blue cheese (including the rind)

Place the yeast in a bowl or jug with the sugar and beer. Stir to mix, then leave to stand in a warm place for 5 minutes. If using fast-action dried yeast there's no need to let it stand.

Sift the flour and salt into a bowl (or that of a stand mixer), then stir in the beer and yeast mixture. It should feel a bit wet and sloppy. Mix well. Add a light dusting of flour to the worktop, then turn out the dough and knead for 10 minutes or until it feels springy and smooth (or for 5–6 minutes using the dough hook in the mixer). Put in a bowl (or keep in the bowl of the mixer), cover tightly with cling film and place somewhere warm (but not above 36°C/96°F) for 1½–3 hours to rise – the time will depend on the temperature of the room and the beer (cold or at room temperature) and on the yeast. I like to place it in a sunny window or near a stove or radiator – basically a warm part of the kitchen. The dough should have more than doubled in size and have some bubbles appearing on top by the end. It should have no spring left when you push it with your finger.

While the dough is rising, cook the onions in the olive oil in a wide pan, uncovered, on a low heat for about 1 hour or until caramelised and rich golden brown, stirring every 5 minutes or so to scrape the bottom of the pan.

Stir the mustard into the caramelised onions.

Uncover and knock the bread back by punching it in, then knead for 1 minute on the worktop. Divide the dough in two and pat out each piece into a round about 25.5cm (10in) in diameter. Place the caramelised onions with mustard and both cheeses in the centre of each round. Bring the edges of the dough into the centre and knead the onions and cheese into the dough for a few seconds – you don't want it to be evenly mixed through, it's lovely just swirled through. Pat out into rounds again.

Flour a baking tray. Turn the loaves upside down, neater side up, and flatten out slightly so that they are about 3cm (1¼in) high. Place side by side on the prepared baking tray, leaving a little space in between each one, then dust the tops with flour and slash a few times on the top with a sharp knife. Cover with a light dry tea towel and place somewhere warm (not above 36°C/96°F) to rise. The loaves should rise to 1½–2 times their original volume and should not be springy when ready – this will take about 45 minutes.

Preheat the oven to 220°C (425°F), Gas mark 7.

Remove the tea towel and transfer the tray very carefully (remembering that the dough will be light and airy, so don't knock them) to the oven and cook for 5 minutes. Turn the oven temperature down to 200°C (400°F), Gas mark 6 and cook for a further 30–40 minutes until the loaves sound hollow when tapped on the base. Cool on a wire rack.

RASPBERRY JELLY

My six-year-old daughter happily proclaimed this as the best recipe in the book, 'or maybe even in the world'. What more can I say?

Serves 3–4

2 leaves of gelatine
100g (3½oz) raspberries (fresh or frozen), plus extra fresh raspberries to serve
60g (2½oz) caster or granulated sugar
juice of ½ lemon

Place the gelatine leaves in a heatproof bowl and cover well with cold water. Allow to sit for 3–5 minutes until completely soft.

Meanwhile, put the raspberries, sugar, lemon juice and 150ml (5fl oz) water in a blender and whiz to combine. Taste and add more sugar or lemon juice if necessary. Pour through a sieve and discard the seeds.

Drain the water from the gelatine and place the gelatine back in the bowl. Pour 2 tablespoons of boiling water (it must be boiling) over the gelatine and stir to dissolve, then pour the raspberry mixture onto the dissolved gelatine, stirring well. Decant into your chosen bowl, individual cups or glasses and place in the fridge for at least 2½ hours, until set.

Serve with fresh whole raspberries and cold, softly whipped cream, or ice cream.

A region dotted with delightful port towns and villages; stunning scenery across mountain and sea; and a natural bounty of produce that has drawn producers from all over Europe to stay and work.

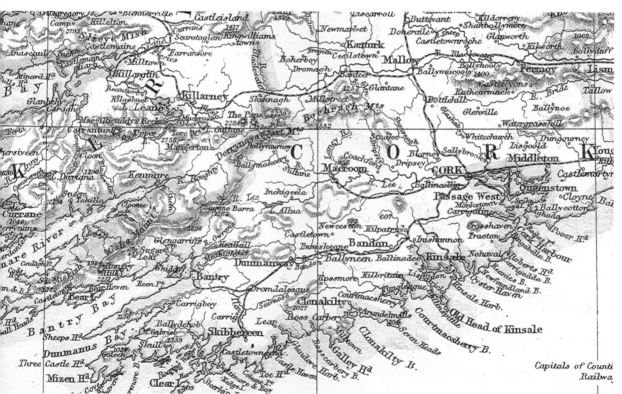

KINSALE

TO

WEST CORK

KINSALE TO WEST CORK

The steady build-up of beauty that Cork is known for is best seen west of Kinsale, which serves as the boundary into storied, sought-after West Cork. From here to the border with Kerry is a region dotted with delightful port towns and villages, stunning scenery across mountain and sea, and a natural bounty of produce that has drawn producers from all over Europe to stay and work.

About 8km south of Kinsale, in the village of Ballinspittle, is Diva Boutique Café & Bakery, a quirky little spot with a vintage feel; tea is served in lovely odd cups and saucers alongside delicious baked goodies like seeded sourdough boule and lemon meringue tart. I love their bread and crisp, fruity pastries, so I sneakily buy a few cakes and hit the road. The contents of that bag of snacks led to my Chocolate pear tart (see pages 116–117) and also my light, fragrant Buttermilk cardamom cake (see page 207) when I wanted to recreate that sense of decadent deliciousness when my travels were at an end.

I'm off again, though, through the bustling market town of Clonakilty and into the striated countryside that has become one of the most desirable places to live in all of Ireland. Near Rosscarbery, I stop to visit Devoy's Organic Farm, an inspirational place abundant with seasonal vegetables and fruit and happy free-ranging livestock. They offer home-grown produce from spinach and kale to onions, courgettes and tomatoes, as well as apples and even blueberries in the summer. Their free-range hens produce organic eggs. All the produce is delivered locally to people who have signed up to the box scheme as well as local restaurants and shops. The sight of fields of burgeoning produce lifts the soul; kale in particular is one of my favourite veggies. Once home, on a cold and blustery day I remember those dark unfurling leaves and my taste buds prickle. Kale is the perfect ingredient for a pesto, and my Kale and hazelnut pesto makes an appearance on Sausage and bean casserole (see page 79) and Potato soup (see page 85) as a seasonal spoonful of zing.

But it's onwards, and the road takes me past the evocative Drombeg Stone Circle, an Iron Age monument with 17 upright stones – it's like West Cork's mini-version of Stonehenge! The two-metre-high sandstone blocks reach up into the blue skies above, standing sentry over the surrounding fields and the sea in the distance, and invite you to stop and admire them. I do, but I confess that the cook in me is especially interested in the *fulachta fiadh*, the cooking pit: I marvel at the fact that our ancestors heated these seemingly ordinary stones and, using them, cooked their meat and even boiled up to seventy gallons of water in just 15 minutes!

No time to test that out, though! I head onwards, driving through the lovely twin villages of Glandore and Union Hall, on either side of an estuary linked by a causeway. A spider's web of tiny rural roads takes me further west along the coast as far as Castletownshend, 12km away, with its quaint 18th-century stone cottages that lead down to the small port.

Not far from here, near Castletownshend, is what I have been heading for. Sally and her daughter Joleine Barnes have won many awards for their wonderful Woodcock Smokery, which is where they smoke wild salmon as well as other sustainable fish. They are dedicated to the ethos of the slow food movement and their fish is smoked using traditional methods with no artificial additives. It is then sold throughout Ireland and in the UK, too. The aromas coming from the gently smoking fish make my mouth water, and so I leave with some beautiful undyed smoked haddock and salmon. Later these two ingredients find their way into my Smokey fishcakes (see page 77).

From Castletownshend, it's 9km north to Skibbereen, West Cork's busiest town. The Taste of West Cork Food Festival takes place here in September, but even now, in early summer, there is a buzz about food, as the region's artisan producers are regular visitors to town, bringing their delicious wares to sell in shops and in markets throughout the year.

On the edge of town, Anthony Boyle and Morgan Hurley's Thornhills Organic Farm is just one such expert producer. Their vegetables and fruit are on sale every Saturday in Skibbereen's farmers' market on Old Market Square, jostling for your attention among many other artisan and seasonal products, including delicious jams and honeys produced by the nearby Knockeen Honey and Fruit Farm. I buy some honey; this purchase later comes to good use to make my Honey and mint buttermilk ice cream (see page 272) extra special!

If I was looking to stay in Skib – as it's referred to locally – my first stop would be Liss Ard Estate, a beautifully restored Georgian country house sitting on 200 acres of stunning countryside. Allow time for their great breakfast before you leave!

From Skibbereen, I head southward to Baltimore, a classic fishing village with a storied past: on 20 June 1631 a band of pirates came ashore and kidnapped over 100 of the townspeople, most of whom were sold into slavery in North Africa. Thankfully, things are much quieter these days – the village comes alive in summer when sailors, kayakers and anglers descend on the village and turn it into a watery playground. The village has a fine dining reputation, maintained by places like Glebe Gardens & Café which uses lavender and herbs picked fresh from the beautiful gardens to enhance the flavours of the food sourced almost exclusively from local producers.

DETOUR: CAPE CLEAR AND SHERKIN ISLANDS

Off the coast of Baltimore are a handful of islands that are popular
with day-trippers. The two most visited are Cape Clear and Sherkin,
which are easily reached by ferry from Baltimore dock. Sherkin Island
is only 10 minutes away and its breathtaking landscapes and golden
beaches make it a mecca for walkers and holidaymakers staying in one of
the island's two pubs, the Islander's Rest. The other pub, the Jolly Roger,
is famed for its hearty seafood chowder.

It takes 45 minutes by ferry to get to Cape Clear, which is an Irish-
speaking haven for bird-lovers; it's a favourite spot for all manner of sea birds,
including Manx shearwater, kittiwakes, gannet, fulmar and guillemot, who
pass here in their tens of thousands. October is the best time to see them.
The rest of the island is a rugged patchwork of pebbly beaches and steep
cliffs covered in gorse and wild flowers – the perfect place to commune with
nature away from the hustle and bustle of the mainland. Also on the island is
the Cape Clear Goat Farm, established by Ed Harper in 1979. Ed makes ice
cream and goat's cheese – and is always on hand to teach you anything you
need to know about goat husbandry and sell you his products.

My destination for the evening is another of the islands off Baltimore's shore,
and once I've finished exploring the town I make my way around the coastline
as far as Cunnamore Pier, from where I board the *Thresher* for the short journey
across to the remote and tranquil Heir Island. On arrival in the sparkling waters
of the harbour I head to Island Cottage restaurant, run by John Desmond
and Ellmary Fenton; John cooks the food while Ellmary takes care of the teeny
weeny dining room. It is very small restaurant, so they offer a set menu, which
usually includes the freshest of fish, duck, beef or lamb as well as shrimp and crab
caught by the island's fishermen. Each table is laid with a basket of their fabulous
bread. John and Ellmary have been going about their business this way for the
last 20 years and it more than works: dinner here is one of the most memorable
experiences I could have anywhere in the country. You'll need to book way ahead
(by phone only) to secure a seat and they're only open in the summertime.

After dinner I bid a fond farewell to John and Ellmary, telling them I'll definitely
be back soon, and board the *Thresher* back to the mainland, watching the caves and
creeks along the island's coastline recede into the distance.

SMOKEY FISHCAKES WITH DILL AND HORSERADISH MAYONNAISE

In Ireland we have an abundance of great smokeries and this recipe is a delicious way of making a little smoked salmon go far. I adore this sweet, hot and mustardy, Scandinavian-style mayonnaise with any smoked fish and it's particularly at home here with these lovely, comforting fishcakes.

Makes 4 large or 8 small fishcakes

50g (2oz) butter
75g (3oz) shallots, peeled and chopped
1 clove of garlic, peeled and crushed
375g (13oz) smoked haddock (ask for undyed), cut into 1cm (½in) dice
100g (3½oz) smoked salmon, finely chopped
½ tsp salt
good twist of black pepper
300g (11oz) cold mashed potato
1 tbsp chopped dill
1 egg, beaten
a little flour (optional)

FOR THE DILL AND HORSERADISH MAYONNAISE
1 egg yolk
1 tbsp Dijon mustard
2 tsp cider vinegar
2 tsp honey
15g (½oz) grated horseradish
1 tbsp chopped dill
pinch of salt
twist of black pepper
100ml (3½fl oz) sunflower oil

First, make the mayonnaise. Put all the ingredients except the sunflower oil into a bowl and whisk to combine. Add the oil in a very slow trickle, whisking constantly (either by hand or using a hand-held electric beater). When all the oil has been added you should have a soft thick consistency. Adjust the seasoning and put in the fridge while you make the fishcakes.

Melt half the butter in a saucepan on a medium heat, add the shallot and garlic, cover the pan and cook for 5–6 minutes until softened. When soft, add the haddock and salmon and season with salt and pepper. Cook, uncovered, stirring frequently, until cooked thoroughly. Leave the fish mixture to cool.

Mix the cold fish with the cold mashed potato. Add the dill and beaten egg and season to taste. Mix again, then form into 4 large or 8 small patties (flour your hands if you need to).

Heat the remaining butter in a frying pan on a medium heat until foaming. Fry the patties for 4–5 minutes on each side until golden brown and hot right through.

Serve the fishcakes with the dill and horseradish mayonnaise and a green salad.

SAUSAGE AND BEAN CASSEROLE WITH KALE AND HAZELNUT PESTO

There ain't nothing delicate about this dish: it's perfectly big and hearty, just ideal for a cold blustery day when you need a hug in a bowl.

Serves 4–6 as a main course

FOR THE CASSEROLE

240g (8½oz) dried haricot beans, soaked in cold water, to cover, overnight, or
    2 x 400g tins, strained (retain the liquid)
2 tbsp extra virgin olive oil
8 large butcher's sausages
3 onions, peeled, halved and sliced
2 cloves of garlic, peeled and crushed or finely grated
salt and freshly ground black pepper
2 x 400g tins of chopped tomatoes
1 sprig of fresh rosemary
2 tsp sugar

FOR THE KALE AND HAZELNUT PESTO

60g (2½oz) hazelnuts
100g (3½oz) kale, curly kale or cavolo nero without stalks, roughly chopped
1 large clove of garlic, peeled and finely crushed or grated
30g (1¼oz) finely grated hard cheese, such as mature Coolea or Parmesan
200ml (7fl oz) extra virgin olive oil, plus 50ml (2fl oz) to cover the pesto in the
    jar
small pinch of salt (optional)

FOR THE RUSTIC CROUTONS

1 small loaf of ciabatta, or sourdough or white yeast bread (a few days old if
    possible)
75–100ml (3–3½fl oz) extra virgin olive oil
sea salt flakes

Continued overleaf.

SAUSAGE AND BEAN CASSEROLE WITH KALE AND HAZELNUT PESTO *Continued*

Preheat the oven to 200°C (400°F), Gas mark 6. Place the hazelnuts on a baking tray and roast in the oven for 4–5 minutes until the nuts under the skin are golden. Put into a tea towel, rub the skins to loosen and then pick out the nuts, discarding the skins. Keep the oven on.

To make the croutons, break the bread into chunks, 3–4cm (1¼–1½in) in size. Place in a bowl, drizzle with the olive oil and season with sea salt flakes. Spread out on a baking tray and cook in the oven for 5–8 minutes until light golden.

Now make the pesto. Put the kale or cavolo nero in a food processor and whiz for a few minutes until quite finely chopped (almost as fine as chopped herbs). Add the garlic, the peeled and roasted hazelnuts and the cheese and whiz until fine. Add the 200ml (7fl oz) olive oil, then taste and add a small pinch of salt if necessary. Pour into a sterilised jar, or 2 small jars, and bang down on the worktop to remove any air bubbles. Pour in the 50ml (2fl oz) olive oil, cover with a lid and put in the fridge. This will keep in the fridge for up to 6 months. To use, pour the olive oil off the top into a clean small bowl, then spoon out the desired amount of pesto. Bang down again on the worktop and clean around the inside of the jar with kitchen paper before pouring the olive oil back in to cover, and store as before.

Drain the soaked beans and place in a saucepan. Cover with fresh cold water, place on a high heat and bring to the boil, then boil for 45–60 minutes until tender. When cooked, strain the beans, reserving the cooking water.

Place ½ tablespoon of the olive oil in a saucepan or flameproof casserole on a medium–high heat and add the sausages. Cook for a few minutes, turning occasionally, until golden on all sides. Take out and slice into 2cm (¾in) pieces, then set aside.

Place the remaining olive oil in the pan and add the onions and garlic. Season with salt and pepper and cook for about 10 minutes, uncovered, stirring occasionally, until the onions are soft and light golden.

Next, return the sausages to the pan with the tomatoes, cooked (or tinned) beans, 300ml (11fl oz) of the bean cooking liquid (or the liquid from the tins, made up to 300ml/11fl oz with water if necessary), the rosemary, sugar and some salt and pepper. Cover and cook on a low heat for 20 minutes, then uncover and cook for a further 20 or so minutes until slightly thicker and the flavours have infused. Season to taste.

Serve the sausage and bean casserole in warm bowls, topped with the rustic croutons and a generous drizzle of the Kale and hazelnut pesto.

BACON AND WHISKEY JAM

Sweet and a bit salty, with a hint of spice: this is completely divine on hot buttered toast at any time of the day.

Makes 2 x 400g (14oz) jars

900g (2lb) rashers of back bacon, cut into strips
10g (scant ½oz) butter (optional)
400g (14oz) shallots, peeled and chopped
2 cloves of garlic, not too large, peeled and chopped
½ tsp sweet smoked paprika
1 tsp ground ginger
½ tsp ground cinnamon
½ tsp ground allspice
150ml (5fl oz) Irish whiskey
100g (3½oz) light soft brown sugar
100g (3½oz) honey
150ml (5fl oz) cider vinegar
100g (3½oz) marmalade

Sterilise two jam jars: wash them in hot soapy water then transfer them to a moderate oven to dry.

Fry the bacon in a wide low-sided sauté pan, stirring frequently, until cooked and beginning to brown. Remove the bacon with a slotted spoon and set aside. If there is a lot of fat in the pan, discard most of it, leaving just enough to sweat the shallots – about 1 tablespoon. If there is not enough fat, add a little knob of butter – about 10g (scant ½oz).

Add the shallots and garlic to the pan and cook gently on a low heat until softened. Then add the spices and cook for a few minutes. Next, add the whiskey, turn up the heat and stir to deglaze the bottom of the pan and cook out most of the alcohol, being very careful as it may flame. Do not measure out the whiskey near the pan or flame.

Finally, return the bacon to the pan, add the sugar, honey, vinegar and marmalade and let it bubble until it becomes sticky and glossy. Transfer into the sterilised jars, allow to cool, then label and store. This will keep for up to 1 month in the fridge.

Serve at room temperature, or even a little warm, on buttered toast.

BACON AND SMOKED HADDOCK RISOTTO WITH PEAS

Rice has a wonderful ability to soak up other flavours, and in this simple risotto the smoked haddock plays a blinder with the salty bacon and sweet peas.

Serves 4–6 as a main course

50g (2oz) butter
250g (9oz) peeled and chopped red onions
3 cloves of garlic, peeled and crushed or finely grated
200g (7oz) bacon, streaky or belly, cut into 0.5 x 2cm (¼ x ¾in) lardons
good pinch of salt
good twist of black pepper
400g (14oz) carnaroli or arborio rice
200ml (7fl oz) white wine or cider
1.5 litres (2½ pints) hot stock (light chicken or vegetable or a light fish stock)
600g (1lb 6oz) smoked haddock, skinned, boned and diced
200ml (7fl oz) double or regular cream
200g (7oz) fresh or frozen peas
100g (3½oz) grated hard cheese, such as a Parmesan or Cheddar type
3 tbsp chopped parsley leaves
juice of ½ lemon

Melt the butter in a pan on a medium heat. Add the onion, garlic and bacon and season with the salt and pepper. Turn the heat down to low, cover and cook for 6–8 minutes, but do not allow them to brown.

Add the rice and cook for a few minutes, stirring to get each grain well coated with butter. Add the wine or cider and cook, uncovered, until it evaporates, stirring continuously. Then add the hot stock little by little – about a ladleful (100ml/3½fl oz) at a time – and cook, stirring, until it is absorbed by the rice. This should take about 15 minutes. The rice should be still slightly firm in the middle but not hard. The risotto should be soft and slightly runny.

While the risotto is cooking, cook the smoked haddock in the cream in a saucepan for a couple of minutes until opaque in the centre, then set aside. When the rice is ready, fold in the haddock cream. Mix in the peas and cheese and cook for a further 2–3 minutes (fresh peas will take a couple of minutes longer to cook). Sprinkle with the parsley and lemon juice, check the seasoning and serve.

POTATO SOUP WITH KALE AND HAZELNUT PESTO

A potato soup is like a great black dress – dress it up, dress it down, it works for any occasion. I love the Kale and hazelnut pesto on everything from roast vegetables to toasted sourdough bread and when drizzled over this velvety potato soup it's a feast in a bowl.

Serves 4–6 as a starter

25g (1oz) butter
1 clove of garlic, peeled and crushed
150g (5oz) chopped onions
250g (9oz) potato, peeled and cut into 1cm (½in) cubes
salt and a good twist of black pepper
800ml (1 pint 9fl oz) hot light chicken or vegetable stock (don't add it all, save
    some to check consistency when blending)
¼ tsp freshly ground nutmeg
100ml (3½fl oz) milk
100ml (3½fl oz) double or regular cream
1–2 tbsp Kale and hazelnut pesto (see pages 79–80), to serve

Put a saucepan on a medium heat, add the butter and allow to melt and foam. Tip in the garlic, onion and potato, stir to combine and season with salt and pepper. Turn the heat down to low and cover the vegetables with a leftover butter wrapper, if you have one (or some greaseproof paper). Cook for 10 minutes, stirring regularly.

Add most of the hot stock and bring to the boil, then season again with salt, pepper and the nutmeg, turn the heat up high and cook until the potatoes are completely tender.

Transfer to a blender and whiz for at least 2–3 minutes, until the soup is velvety.

Meanwhile, rinse out the saucepan and return the soup to it when blended, through a sieve if you wish. Add the milk and cream, adjust the seasoning and add more stock if necessary. It should be thick but not gloopy. Serve in warm bowls with a drizzle of Kale and hazelnut pesto. Enjoy.

GOOSEBERRY TART

A fruit tart is about as Irish as it gets. Every cook in a pub or home would have their own recipe and when served with lots of softly whipped cream and a nice scattering of brown sugar, it's hard to beat.

Serves 6

250g (9oz) plain flour, plus extra for dusting
1 tbsp icing sugar
125g (4½oz) unsalted butter, plus 15g (½oz) for buttering the plate
2 tbsp sour cream or crème fraîche
550g (1¼lb) gooseberries, topped and tailed (you can use frozen fruit)
125g (4½oz) brown sugar (demerara or light muscovado), plus 3 tbsp for
    sprinkling
1 small egg, beaten
softly whipped cream, to serve

First make the pastry. Sift the flour and icing sugar into a bowl and rub in the 125g (4½oz) butter until it resembles coarse breadcrumbs. Add the sour cream or crème fraîche and bring together to form a dough. Lightly flour the worktop. Turn out the dough and pat into a round about 1cm (½in) thick. Wrap in baking parchment or cling film and place in the fridge to chill for at least 30 minutes, but it would also be fine to use the next day, or even to freeze it.

Preheat the oven to 180°C (350°F), Gas mark 4. Butter an ovenproof plate with the remaining butter.

Roll out the pastry with a dusting of flour on top and underneath to a 28cm (11in) round. Transfer the pastry to the buttered plate, letting the excess tip over the sides. Place the gooseberries in a heap in the centre of the pastry and scatter the 125g (4½oz) brown sugar over the top. Bring the pastry in from the sides and tuck into the centre – it will not cover all the gooseberries. Brush the pastry with some beaten egg and sprinkle with 2 tablespoons of brown sugar. Bake for 45–55 minutes until golden on top and the goosberries are tender.

Sprinkle with the remaining sugar and serve with softly whipped cream.

IRISH RHUBARB CAKE

A delicious way to use rhubarb, this is the kind of recipe that's been made in Ireland for over a century with whatever fruit is in season. Try it in winter using sweet eating apples.

Serves 6

225g (8oz) plain flour
½ tsp baking powder
100g (3½oz) unsalted butter
1 egg, beaten
75ml (3fl oz) milk
300g (11oz) chopped rhubarb
100g (3½oz) caster sugar, plus 2 tbsp for sprinkling

Preheat the oven to 180°C (350°F), Gas mark 4.

Sift the flour and baking powder into a bowl, then rub in the butter until it resembles breadcrumbs. Mix the egg and milk together, then add to the flour and combine to form a soft dough. It is supposed to be wet.

Spread a thin layer in a shallow 1 litre (1¾ pint) pie dish, to a depth of about 5mm (¼in).

Mix the rhubarb and the 100g (3½oz) sugar and pile it into the dish, then spoon the rest of the dough over and spread it slightly – don't worry, it will join up in the oven. Sprinkle the 2 tablespoons of sugar over the top and bake in the oven for 40–50 minutes until the top is golden and crunchy and a skewer inserted into the centre finds the fruit tender. Serve with softly whipped cream.

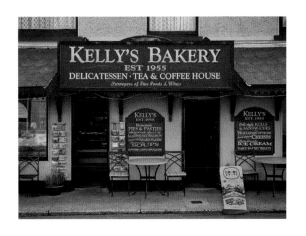

I leave with a few picnic provisions for the journey and I travel deeper into the peninsula. The landscape becomes wilder as I travel westward and around the tip.

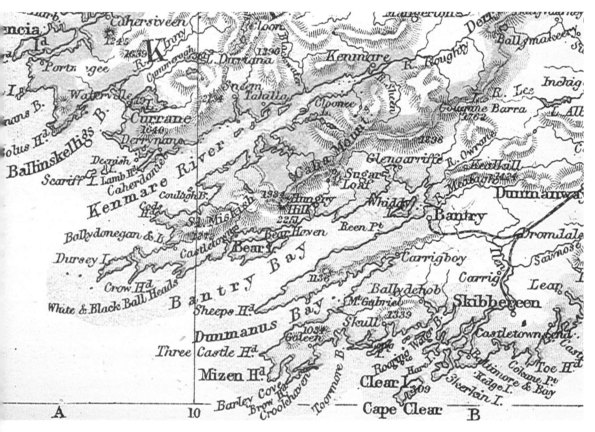

MIZEN

SHEEP'S HEAD
AND BEARA

MIZEN, SHEEP'S HEAD AND BEARA

The next morning I say goodbye to briny Baltimore and head west again, destination Ballydehob, the gateway to the Mizen Peninsula.

From here, I head to the charming village of Schull, where, less than 2km out of town, lies Tom and Giana Ferguson's Gubbeen Farm. The fabulous Ferguson family are notorious for their wonderful, award-winning, soft, rinded cheese called Gubbeen, which comes in various sizes, and also a smoked version, but their talents do not end there. The family-run business produces greens (grown by their daughter Clovisse), meat products (courtesy of their son Fingal) and also oatcakes, which are the perfect accompaniment to their cheese. The beautiful chorizo made by Fingal inspired my West Cork paella (see pages 98–101), and the Gubbeen cheese is the perfect complement for any cheese board.

Of course, I leave with a few picnic provisions for the journey and I travel deeper into the peninsula. The landscape becomes wilder as I travel westward and around the tip. On the one side there's the odd stone house lying derelict and crumbling in a field, while on the other the view stretches out to sea, far beyond the shoreline and the sparkling blue waters; I can see Cape Clear and, beyond it, the Fastnet Lighthouse, a lone sentry on a rock in the middle of the ocean – its Irish name, Carraig Aonar, suits it well: the lonely rock.

DETOUR: BROW HEAD

The Irish mainland's southernmost point and the spot from which Guglielmo Marconi transmitted his very first radio message that received a reply in 1904 to Cornwall, is on Brow Head. It's easy enough to get there: from Crookhaven, Brow Head is marked along a narrow track to the left; I park my car at the bottom and walk the rest of the way. I can't imagine anywhere else more remote on the island, with only the sound of the sea and the gulls to accompany me.

One of my favourite places in Mizen is the beach at Barleycove, a broad stretch of sand sheltered between two bluffs, where sand dunes rise and fall as far as the eye can see. It is a beautiful, calm beach, which has been designated a Special Area of Conservation because of the variety of wildlife that inhabits it. I park the car by the causeway and walk across the pontoon down to the beach, where I sit in the dunes for a bit and enjoy some Gubbeen cheese, salami and oatcakes. When I think back on my visit there I decide that my picnic was perfect, but next time I'll bring along a dollop of chutney, and perhaps my Cheesy buttermilk scones (see page 114). Later, I remember that picnic and it comes to me in a flash – fish, for a

picnic by the sea. And hey presto, my Rustic salmon pâté (see page 108) is born!

Fuelled by my Gubbeen picnic I'm ready for a walk on Three Castle Head, another gem of the Mizen Peninsula. To get to the ruins of Dunlough Castle, with its cliff-top lake and sea views, I need to walk through the farm of the Ungerer family where Lucas and Joanne Ungerer have recently opened a lovely café (open from mid-June to September) selling great sandwiches, coffee and freshly baked scones. This is the perfect stop to rest and eat, among the crumbling walls of the 13th-century castle; it has to be one of the most remote and stunning places in the world, it is no wonder that there are no historical records of this fortress built by the O'Mahoney clan ever being attacked! It is perfectly situated in a valley which still allows you breathtaking views on a clear day over the Dunmanus Bay and the seemingly never-ending waters of the Atlantic.

Back on the road, I'm heading along the northern edge of the peninsula as far as Durrus, whose gourmet reputation far exceeds the size of the town. This is all thanks to artisan producers like Jeffa Gill of Durrus Farmhouse cheese, who began producing her award-winning raw milk cheese in 1979 and has since added two others to her original recipe – Durrus Óg and Dunmanus. The former is a young cheese, aged only for 10 days, the latter a semi-hard cheese which is aged for at least three months. All three are made seasonally from the cows from two farms when they are out at pasture, so you have to catch it while you can!

Cheese bought, I head back into town and call into Carmel Summers at the Good Things Café. An excellent lunch follows, even if I'm torn between which dish to pick: will it be the carpaccio of John Dory or the lamb with mint pilaf?

Besides being a foodie haven, Durrus is also a convenient access to the second peninsula I plan to explore. Sheep's Head is the smallest and least visited of Cork's three peninsulas, and it's aptly named: by far the biggest sign of life I saw was of the woolly kind, white, cloud-like shapes dotted around the fields that stretch as far as the eye can see. Halfway along the peninsula is Ahakista, and as I travel beyond this village the landscapes become wild and beautiful, but really it's all about the sea views, which are simply spectacular. There's another small village about 6km southwest of Ahakista, but once I pass Kilcrohane it's just me and the sheep … and the views.

I work my way around the peaceful peninsula and find myself arriving in busy Bantry, set at the head of the magnificent bay. I pay a visit to Bantry House, which has been in the White family since 1729 – it was Richard White who played a key role in Irish history in 1798 when he warned local authorities of the imminent arrival of the French fleet in the bay – and wander through its gorgeous Italianate gardens, ambling through the formal gardens, weaving through the box-lined paths underneath a cascade of beautiful wisteria in full, show-stopping bloom. The tearoom calls me, the aroma of baking cakes and scones lures me in, but alas I must press on! I make a mental note that on my return home I will have the scones I missed out on here, but I fancy something savoury, so Cheesy buttermilk scones it is (see page 114), warm from the oven, light of crumb and slathered with melting Irish butter.

About 6km north of Bantry, in the small village of Ballylickey, is Manning's Emporium which started life 70 years ago as a post office but is now a treasure trove of West Cork's gourmet offerings. Inside I find produce from all over the region – cheeses, cured meats, home-brewed wines and local vegetables, the shelves overflowing with seasonal and artisan treats. I get distracted by the timetable of foodie events the deli is hosting, from how to make pizza in a wood-burning oven to sherry tastings! I struggle back to the car with a well-stocked hamper and I'm off again, ready to explore Beara.

DETOUR: GARINISH ISLAND

Glengariff, on the edge of the Beara Peninsula, is the departure point for the 10-minute boat journey to Garinish Island, also known as Ilnacullin. The island benefits from a subtropical microclimate. At the turn of the 20th century this unique microclimate encouraged the island's owner, Annan Bryce, to commission English landscape architect Harold Peto to design a formal Italianate garden and fill it with colourful camellias, magnolias and rhododendrons. It is a surprising taste of the Mediterranean in the middle of Western Ireland, and no less impressive for it. There's also a Martello tower built in 1805 (the view from the top is glorious) and a Grecian temple, as well as a charming café.

In exploring Beara, I'm confronted with lots of options. I can do the whole 137km loop road, which takes me past the fishing villages of the southern coast and out to the tip of the peninsula. From there I can get to Dursey Island via the cable car (the only one in the country!) before looping back around the northern edge with its spectacular countryside cut through by a rural road that wends its way past some pretty gorgeous views. Along the way, I could stop and visit the always inspirational Veronica Steele in her farm just outside Eyries, on the southern edge of the peninsula. It was back in 1976 that she first made the Milleens Cheese her farm is now famous for – the first artisan farmhouse cheese made in Ireland – and which we still serve at Ballymaloe. Its fantastic flavours need no supplementing, try with a local honey and some warm crusty bread.

I say goodbye to Veronica and turn back towards Adrigole, where I begin cutting my way northwards through the heart of the peninsula. I'm sorry to miss out on Dursey (I'll get there again) but my reward is another scenic blockbuster, the Healy Pass, which rises to 334m as it snakes through the Caha Mountains.

The pass also marks the boundary between counties Cork and Kerry. My destination is the Park Hotel in Kenmare, right on the edge of town, overlooking Kenmare Bay. It's been in the hotel business since 1897, and practice makes perfect. Before I get there I make one final stop: I heed the call of my sweet tooth and let my eyes feast on the chocolatey goodness on display at Lorge Chocolates about 5km south of town, where French master chocolatier Benoit Lorge makes some of the best chocolates I've ever tasted! The aroma of the chocolates hits you as you enter the shop, with truffles, liqueurs, nougats and fruit pieces dipped in chocolate. The combination of chocolate and fruit is always a winner for me, and makes an appearance in my Chocolate pear tart (see pages 116–117). I tear myself away from chocolate heaven, but not before stashing a few truffles into my bag for an after-dinner treat!

WEST CORK PAELLA

When on holidays in Spain I always have to have paella at least once. I adore
a *paella mixta*, with both meat and fish, and the more variety the better. Paella
is the ultimate dish for entertaining a crowd and is so flexible – it can contain
meat, fish, shellfish or game, depending on what's available. When I make paella
at home I can never resist throwing in some of Fingal Furguson's delicious
Gubbeen chorizo for an extra kick of flavour.

Serves 4–6 as a main course

200g (7oz) prepared pork belly or streaky pork (all bones and rind removed), cut
 into 1 x 2cm (½ x ¾in) pieces
1 tsp smoked paprika
extra virgin olive oil
pinch of salt
250g (9oz) onions, peeled and chopped
4 fat cloves of garlic, peeled and sliced
150g (5oz) chorizo, peeled if cured (soft, fresh chorizo doesn't need peeling),
 halved lengthways and thinly sliced at an angle
350g (12oz) paella rice (if you can't get any, you can at a push use risotto rice
 instead)
200ml (7fl oz) cider
800–900ml (1 pint 9fl oz–1 pint 11fl oz) hot chicken stock
200g (7oz) monkfish, trimmed and cut into 1cm (½in) slices, or 200g (7oz)
 scallops and their corals, trimmed
150g (5oz) fresh or frozen peas
150g (5oz) 2 medium peppers, roasted (see page 48)
2–3 tbsp chopped parsley leaves
1 wedge of lemon per person

Preheat the oven to 180°C (350°F), Gas mark 4. Rub the pork with the smoked
paprika and 2 teaspoons of olive oil. Put on a baking tray and roast for 20–25
minutes, turning the pieces over halfway through.

   While the pork is roasting, put 2 tablespoons of olive oil, the onion, garlic and
chorizo in a wide, low-sided pan or paella pan. Cook on a medium heat until the
onion is translucent and colouring at the edges.

Continued overleaf.

WEST CORK PAELLA *Continued*

Next, add the rice and cook, stirring gently, for a few minutes, to coat the grains with the oil in the pan. Pour in the cider, shake the pan and allow the rice to absorb the liquid. Then add a quarter of the hot stock and allow to bubble and absorb. Add a further quarter of the liquid along with the cooked pork. When the second lot of stock is absorbed, test the rice – it should still have a bit of resistance at the core. Add the fish and a further quarter of the stock. When it is absorbed the rice should be nearly cooked with a very slight firmness in the centre.

Add the peas and roasted peppers and as much more of the stock as necessary to loosen the paella to a soft state. Give the pan a little shake, bring up to a bubble, then pop a lid on and cook for a couple of minutes (fresh peas will take a minute or two longer than frozen). Season to taste with salt and pepper.

To serve, sprinkle with the parsley, drizzle with 2 tablespoons of olive oil and add the lemon wedges.

COCKLES WITH CHORIZO, ROSEMARY AND CREAM

A delicious and quick way to prepare cockles using the magical combination of chorizo, rosemary and cream. Best eaten as soon as it's made.

Serves 4 as a starter, or 2 as a main, with salad and crusty bread

150g (5oz) chorizo, peeled if cured (soft, fresh chorizo doesn't need peeling) and
  cut into small dice (less than 1cm/½in)
2 tsp chopped rosemary leaves
1 x 400g tin of chopped tomatoes
1 tsp caster sugar
40–48 cockles in their shells (10–12 per person), well washed and scrubbed –
  discard any that are not tightly shut or don't close when tapped
150ml (5fl oz) double or regular cream

Put the chorizo and rosemary into a pan, then put on a low to medium heat and cook until the oil from the chorizo runs and it begins to sizzle. Add the tomatoes, sugar and cockles, place the lid on the pan, turn up the heat and allow the cockles to open. This will take a few minutes and a few shakes of the pan. Remove the cockles as they open and divide among hot bowls. Discard any cockles that remain closed.

Add the cream to the tomatoes and chorizo and allow to bubble and thicken slightly, then pour over the cockles and serve.

PAN-FRIED JOHN DORY WITH PICKLED GINGER BEURRE BLANC

A twist on the classic beurre blanc, this ginger sauce is one of the best accompaniments for a stunning piece of meaty pan-fried John Dory.

Serves 4 as a main course

softened butter, for greasing
4 x 150g (5oz) fillets of John Dory (double fillets, from 2 fish)
salt and freshly ground black pepper

FOR THE PICKLED GINGER BEURRE BLANC
1 tbsp chopped shallot
1 tbsp pickled ginger, coarsely chopped
3 tbsp white wine
3 tbsp white wine vinegar
2 tbsp juice from the pickled ginger jar, plus a little more if necessary
1 tbsp double or regular cream
175g (6oz) cold butter, cut into 1–2cm (½–¾in) cubes
1 tbsp pickled ginger, very finely chopped

First make the pickeld ginger buerre blanc. Put the shallot, pickled ginger, wine, vinegar and the juice from the ginger in a saucepan. Place on a medium heat, uncovered, and reduce to 1 tablespoon liquid. Add the cream, bring to the boil and allow it to thicken very slightly. Take off the heat and leave to cool until the sides of the pan are cool enough to touch, but still slightly warm.

Return the pan to a very low heat and whisk in the cold butter, two or three pieces at a time. Allow each piece to melt and emulsify before adding the next. When all the butter is in the sauce, strain it into a warm but not hot bowl.

Add the very finely chopped pickled ginger and a little more juice if necessary, then set the bowl somewhere warm – I sit it in hot but not boiling water in a saucepan. If you're serving it a while later, place the saucepan on a low heat to warm the water, but don't let it boil or the sauce will split. Kept at the right temperature, it can keep warm for a few hours.

Spread the softened butter onto both sides of fish fillet and season. Pan-fry the buttered John Dory, flesh side down, in a hot dry pan for a few minutes, then flip over on to the skin side and cook for 2–3 minutes more. The fillets should be golden and moist, and cooked through to the middle. Spoon the sauce over to serve.

ROAST COD WITH WHITE BEAN AND CHORIZO MASH

I love this quick-to-throw-together mash with roasted fish. The smoked paprika-infused chorizo sausage is one of my favourite ingredients to use in cooking and particularly so when paired with fish. Feel free to use any other round white fish place of the cod.

Serves 4 as a main course

4 x 175g (6oz) thick cod pieces, all bones removed, skin still attached
2 tbsp extra virgin olive oil, plus extra for oiling the fish
salt and freshly ground black pepper
240g (8½oz) dried cannellini beans (or other white beans), soaked in cold water, to cover, overnight, or 2 x 400g tins, strained (retain the liquid)
2 tbsp extra virgin olive oil
2 sprigs of fresh rosemary, leaves stripped and chopped
125g (4½oz) chorizo, peeled if cured (soft, fresh chorizo doesn't need peeling), quartered lengthways and sliced
2 cloves of garlic, peeled and crushed or finely grated
4 tbsp white wine or dry sherry
1 tbsp chopped parsley leaves
lemon wedges and parsley sprigs, to serve

Rub the cod with a little olive oil, season with salt and pepper and set aside.

Drain the soaked beans and place in a saucepan. Cover with cold water, put on a high heat and bring to the boil, then reduce the heat and simmer for 45 minutes–1 hour until tender. Strain in a colander over a heatproof bowl, saving the cooking liquid. Return the beans to the pan (or put the strained tinned beans in the pan).

Preheat the oven to 220°C (425°F), Gas mark 7. Place a heavy griddle pan or an ovenproof frying pan on a high heat and allow to get very hot, almost smoking.

Meanwhile, in a small saucepan, warm the olive oil, then add the rosemary, chorizo and garlic and cook gently until softened, but don't brown. Mash the beans and season. Add the wine or sherry and a few tablespoons of the reserved bean cooking liquid (or liquid from the tins) to create a soft mash. Pour off some of the chorizo oil and save. Add the parsley and the contents of the chorizo pan to the mash, mix and heat through.

Cook the cod, skin side up, on the preheated griddle or frying pan on a high heat for 3–5 minutes until golden underneath, then turn the fish over and pop it into the oven for a further 4–8 minutes, depending on the thickness of the fish. You want the cod to be glistening and flaky inside but not dry.

Place a good dollop of the bean mash on each plate, top with a fish fillet and drizzle with some of the reserved chorizo oil. Serve with a leafy green salad.

RUSTIC SALMON PÂTÉ

I love a delicious pâté, and none more so than this one, which is made up of both fresh and smoked salmon and lots of grated fresh nutmeg all brought together with, of course, lovely salty butter.

Serves 4–6 as a starter

85g (3¼oz) skinned smoked salmon, cut into 1cm (½in) dice
85g (3¼oz) skinned fresh salmon, cut into 1cm (½in) dice
3 tsp chopped dill
3 tsp chopped capers
1 tbsp lemon juice
pinch of salt
twist of black pepper
¼ tsp freshly grated nutmeg
1 clove of garlic, peeled and finely grated or crushed
50g (2oz) crème fraîche
50g (2oz) cream cheese

Put both the salmons with 1 tablespoon of water in a small saucepan with a tight-fitting lid on a low heat and cook for a few minutes until the fish has changed colour the whole way through, making sure not to let it burn.

Mash the fish with a fork, then mix together with all the remaining ingredients. Taste and check the seasoning. Serve on crusty toast.

ROASTED ONIONS

These were a revelation to me the first time I ate them, at my parents-in-law's home. Who knew that onions roasted in their skins with absolutely nothing done to them could be so completely divine? A delicious accompaniment to roast meat, they are also good with some watercress butter melting over the top.

Serves 4 as a side dish

4 onions, unpeeled
watercress butter, to serve (see page 125)

Preheat the oven to 220°C (425°F), Gas mark 7.

Place the unpeeled onions on a roasting tray and roast in the oven for 1 hour or until they feel soft inside.

To eat, cut away the root and squeeze out the soft sweet onion. Serve with watercress butter, if you like.

ROASTED CELERY

I love the enhanced celery flavour that comes from roasting this much under-estimated vegetable. Delicious with fish or a Sunday roast.

Serves 4 as a side dish

10–12 sticks of celery, trimmed
2–3 tbsp extra virgin olive oil
salt and freshly ground black pepper

Preheat the oven to 220°C (425°F), Gas mark 7.

If the celery stalks from the outside of the bunch are large, it's a good idea to blanch them in boiling salted water for just 2 minutes after cutting them. Drain, then dry on kitchen paper.

Cut the celery stalks at an angle into pieces 8–10cm (3¼–4in) in length. Place in a bowl, drizzle with olive oil, season with salt and pepper and toss to coat.

Lay the celery out in a single layer in a roasting tray and roast for 10 minutes or until slightly golden around the edges and almost tender but still with a bit of a bite. Serve.

LAMB BROTH WITH HARICOT BEANS

This dish showcases two lovley ingredients: Irish lamb and dark, leafy kale.
A nourishing and hearty broth for the winter days.

Serves 4 as a main course

120g (4¼oz) dried haricot beans, soaked in cold water, to cover, overnight, or
  1 x 400g tin of haricot beans, strained (retain the liquid)
2 tbsp extra virgin olive oil
200g/7oz onion, peeled and finely chopped
2 cloves of garlic, peeled and finely chopped
salt and freshly ground black pepper
2 sticks of celery, trimmed and chopped into 1cm (½in) dice
250g (9oz) carrots, peeled and chopped into 1cm (½in) dice
175g (6oz) leftover cooked lamb, sliced into 0.5 x 2cm (¼ x ¾in) pieces
550ml (19fl oz) lamb or chicken stock
1 tbsp pesto, such as Kale and hazelnut (see pages 79–80), parsley or basil pesto

Drain the soaked beans and place in a saucepan. Cover with cold water, place
on a high heat and bring to the boil, then boil for 45–60 minutes until tender.
Strain the beans and save 200ml (7fl oz) of the cooking liquid.

Place a large saucepan on a medium heat and add the olive oil. Tip in the onion
and garlic and season with salt and pepper, then cover the pan and cook on a low
heat for 5 minutes or until soft. Add the celery and carrots and cook for 7–10
minutes until just soft. Add the lamb, beans, stock and bean cooking liquid (or
200ml/7fl oz liquid from the tinned beans) and bring to the boil, then turn the
heat down and simmer for 15 minutes until all the flavours have mingled. Season
to taste with salt and pepper.

Serve in warm bowls with a drizzle of pesto over the top.

BUTTERNUT SQUASH BARLEY RISOTTO WITH CHORIZO

The delicious chorizo sausage lends its rusty amber colours and deep paprika flavours to the humble barley, which makes a great risotto-style dish that's very at home on a plate with pan-grilled fish.

Serves 4–6 as a side dish

1 x 720g (1lb 9oz) small butternut squash (about 425g/15oz when prepared), peeled, deseeded and chopped into 1–2cm (½–¾in) cubes
2 tbsp olive oil
200g (7oz) chorizo, peeled if cured (soft, fresh chorizo doesn't need peeling) and cut into 5mm (¼in) slices
1 onion, peeled and finely chopped
salt and freshly ground black pepper
300g (11oz) pearl barley
1 litre (1¾ pints) chicken or vegetable stock
2 tsp chopped rosemary leaves

Preheat the oven to 220°C (425°F), Gas mark 7.

Toss the butternut squash cubes in the olive oil, then put on a baking tray and roast in the oven for 20 minutes or until soft.

Put the chorizo in a dry frying pan on a low heat and cook until the fat renders out. Transfer to a plate, leaivng the oil in the pan, then add the onion to the pan, season with salt and pepper and sweat for 5 minutes. Return the chorizo to the pan, add the pearl barley and cook for 2 minutes. Add the stock and bring to the boil, then cook, uncovered, for 30 minutes, or until the pearl barley is just cooked.

Gently stir through the roasted butternut squash and rosemary and heat through, then season to taste and serve.

CHEESY BUTTERMILK SCONES

A delicious accompaniment to a big bowl of soup or eaten just on their own with a good slathering of salty Irish butter. Watch these disappear very quickly.

Makes 14 scones

450g (1lb) plain flour, plus extra for dusting
1 tsp baking powder
1½ tsp salt
½ tsp cayenne pepper
1 level kitchen tsp* bread soda (or bicarbonate of soda)
75g (3oz) butter
100g (3½oz) Cheddar cheese, grated
350ml (12fl oz) buttermilk

Preheat the oven to 220°C (425°F), Gas mark 7. Dust a baking tray with flour.

Sift the flour, baking powder, salt, cayenne and soda into a bowl and mix with your hands.

Rub in the butter, then mix in the grated cheese. Make a well in the centre and add in all the buttermilk (if the buttermilk is quite thick you may need 25ml/1fl oz more). Using your hand outstretched to resemble a claw, go around the sides of the bowl to mix the wet and dry ingredients. Stop mixing once it all comes together.

Lightly flour the worktop. Tip the dough out onto it, dust more flour over the top and pat the dough into a piece about 2.5cm (1in) high. Cut into 14 'scones', each about 7.5cm (3in) in diameter. Do be careful not to knead the dough at all, otherwise the scones will be tough and heavy.

Place on the prepared baking tray and bake for 10 minutes, then turn the oven temperature down to 200°C (400°F), Gas mark 6 and bake for a further 5 minutes or until the scones are golden and sound hollow when tapped on the base.

*Always ensure you accurately measure out your bread soda using measuring spoons

CHOCOLATE PEAR TART

Crumbly, buttery sweet shortcrust pastry encasing a rich chocolate filling and juicy poached pears – this tart is a treat.

Serves 6–8

FOR THE PASTRY
250g (9oz) plain flour, plus extra for
    dusting
1 tbsp icing sugar
pinch of salt
125g (4½oz) unsalted butter, diced
1 egg, beaten

FOR THE PEARS
3 medium pears, not too soft, peeled,
    quartered and cored
2 tbsp caster sugar

FOR THE CHOCOLATE
200g (7oz) dark chocolate
150g (5oz) unsalted butter
2 whole eggs, plus 3 egg yolks
40g (1½oz) caster sugar

To make the pastry, sift the flour, icing sugar and salt into a bowl and rub in the butter until it resembles coarse breadcrumbs. Add enough of the beaten egg to bring it together to form a dough, reserving any leftover egg for later. Lightly flour the worktop. Turn out the dough and pat into a round about 1cm (½in) thick, then cover with cling film and place in the fridge to chill for at least 30 minutes (or it could be refrigerated overnight, or frozen, too).

You will need a 25.5cm (10in) tart tin with a removable base, with sides 3cm (1¼in) high. When you are ready to roll out the pastry, remove it from the fridge and place between two sheets of cling film (each larger in size than your tart tin). Using a rolling pin, roll the pastry out to no thicker than 5mm (¼in). Make sure to keep it in a round shape as well as large enough to line both the base and the sides of the tin.

Remove the top layer of cling film, slide your hand, palm upwards, under the bottom layer of cling film, then flip the pastry over (so that the cling film is now on top) and carefully lower it into the tart tin. Press the pastry into the edges of the tin (with the cling film still attached) and, using your thumb, 'cut' the pastry along the edge of the tin for a neat finish. Remove the cling film and chill the pastry in the fridge for a further 30 minutes, or in the freezer for 10 minutes (it can keep for weeks like this, covered, in the freezer and can be cooked from frozen but will take an extra couple of minutes to cook).

Preheat the oven to 180°C (350°F), Gas mark 4.

Remove the pastry from the fridge and line with greaseproof paper or baking parchment, leaving plenty to come just above the sides of the tin. Fill with baking beans or dried pulses (all of which can be reused repeatedly), then place in the oven and bake 'blind' for 20–25 minutes until the pastry feels almost dry on the bottom. Take out of the oven and remove the baking beans and paper. Brush the bottom of the pastry with the leftover beaten egg, if there is any, then bake for a further 3 minutes without the paper and beans, until lightly golden. Remove from the oven and set aside. Leave the oven on.

Meanwhile, put the pears in a saucepan with the sugar and 2 tablespoons of water. Cover with a disc of baking parchment and a lid and cook gently on a medium–low heat for 20–30 minutes until tender. Slice the pears thinly and arrange in a single layer over the baked pastry case when ready – arrange these nicely as they may be visible once the tart is cooked.

Put the chocolate and butter in a heatproof bowl over a pan of simmering water. Don't allow the water to get too hot or the chocolate may burn. Take the saucepan off the heat once the water comes to the boil and leave the chocolate and butter to slowly melt. While the chocolate is melting, whisk together the whole eggs, egg yolks and sugar for 5 minutes until fluffy. Then fold in the melted chocolate and butter mixture.

Cover the pears with the chocolate mix and bake in the oven for 7 minutes exactly. It will look slightly unset when it comes out but will set as it cools, over the next hour.

Once the tart has cooled, serve in slices with some softly whipped cream.

My memories of this part of Ireland inspire me to create simpler food — seeing the hard life that the monks endured, and the windswept lands of the villages that didn't survive the Famine.

RING OF KERRY

CO. KERRY

THE RING OF KERRY

When you think of picture-postcard Irish scenery, you're most likely thinking of the Iveragh Peninsula, better known to millions of visitors as the Ring of Kerry – even if that really just refers to the 179km circuit around the peninsula. This is the longest of Ireland's circular routes and easily the most popular: during the busy summer season the tour buses wend their way around the ring in an anti-clockwise direction, the passengers' faces caught in perpetual gasps of wonder as they watch the constantly changing but always spectacular scenery.

I say goodbye to Kenmare and carry on with my trip. Thankfully, unlike buses, cars aren't obliged to do the ring anticlockwise, so I'll still be able to experience the whole of the ring and finish on the right side of it for my onward journey north to County Limerick.

DETOUR: 32KM OF STUNNING SCENERY

Because I'm travelling west, I'm missing out on one of the most spectacularly scenic roads in the whole country. The 32km stretch of switchback roads between Killarney and Kenmare is worth every effort for the feast of fine views. The most famous of these is Ladies' View, about 18km from Killarney. The vista is so named because apparently when Queen Victoria visited here in 1861, her ladies-in-waiting were so taken by the view of the lakes and the mountains around them that the spot was named after them. Another great viewpoint is at Moll's Gap, from which you can see the Macgillycuddy's Reeks mountains rising up on the horizon, swathed in low-lying clouds as they scurry across the summer sky. The viewpoint gets its name from Moll Kissane, who ran an illegal shebeen (drinking establishment) here when the road was being built in the 1820s – it must have been thirsty work indeed!

I could spend days on the Ring of Kerry, such is the wealth of things to see and do, but time is a constraint so I need to be disciplined! From Moll's Gap I head down the mountain to Sneem, where I pay a visit to both Kieran Burns and Peter O'Sullivan, two butchers who've been making the famous Sneem Black Pudding by hand for generations. I wouldn't attempt to recreate something that has taken years to perfect, so instead of creating my own recipe for black pudding I think about all the delicious dishes that could accompany it. At home I experiment with Potato and rosemary soda focaccia for a brunch (see page 133), or Potato and sage gratin for a hearty supper (see page 130).

Halfway between Sneem and Waterville, I turn off by the Scariff Inn in Caherdaniel and make my way past the picture-perfect views of Kenmare Bay and its islands and, beyond it, Bantry Bay. The views are fabulous, and it's hard to tear myself away, but there's plenty more to see and do, so head on I must.

Just a short way down the road is the ferry port for the Skellig Islands, where 1,000 years ago monks committed to finding the ultimate remote retreat in which to practise their religion eked out a hardy living in six sandstone beehive huts virtually perched on the bare rocks. Skellig Michael is, deservedly, a UNESCO World Heritage Site and well worth the choppy crossing, but make sure you have decent footwear: the steps up to the top of the rock demand that you be as sure-footed as possible! If ornithology is your thing, Small Skellig, Michael's neighbour, is home to the second-largest colony of gannets in the world – around 27,000 pairs of them!

It's time for some lunch. The Point Seafood Bar at Renard Point, just outside Cahirsiveen (where you can catch the ferry for Valentia Island), serves excellent fish, lobster and crab, alongside homemade breads, while in Waterville The Smugglers Inn is a fine restaurant and B&B in a 19th-century farmhouse – they do great things with fish, but also serve a mean steak! Decisions, decisions …

DETOUR: THE SKELLIG RING

Another ring within the bigger ring, the 18km detour off the N70 is a roundabout way of getting from Waterville to Portmagee via an Irish-speaking *Gaelteacht*. There are some pretty spectacular views (especially of Skellig Michael), a nice art gallery on the site of a village abandoned during the Famine (Siopa Cill Rialaig, Dun Geagan) and the ruins of a medieval priory at Ballinskelligs built by the same monks who built the beehive huts on Skellig Michael.

Just beyond Cahirveen, near the beautiful beach at Glenbeigh, is Rolf's Fine Foods, another local producer with an award-winning reputation. Here they use homegrown ingredients like strawberries, tomatoes, courgettes and peppers to make a fine range of jams, chutneys and vinegar: I pick up a couple of bottles of their fruit-flavoured vinegar, to experiment with salad dressings.

I'm nearly at the end of my journey for the day. Killorglin, my last stop on the ring, is at its busiest in mid-August when it hosts one of Ireland's most distinctive festivals, Puck Fair, which sees a billy goat (*poc*, in Irish) crowned king for three days while everybody celebrates until the wee hours. It's a wonderful taste of Irish folklore and hospitality, the town buzzes with excitement, noise and festivity, and good food and drink are on offer in abundance. If you're looking for a nice bite in town on any other day, though, I'd recommend Bianconi, which serves local

favourites such as braised lamb shank, the local catch of the day, regional cheeses and smoked fish to an always appreciative clientele! My memories of this part of Ireland inspire me to create simpler food – seeing the hard life that the monks endured, and the windswept lands of the villages that didn't survive the Famine, I rustle up a hearty Irish stew with pearl barley (see page 129) and a simple Honey and almond cake (see pages 134–135) to finish.

PAN-FRIED FISH WITH WATERCRESS BUTTER

Being able to pan-fry a piece of fish is a great skill to have. Try to get the freshest fish possible, preheat your pan really well, butter and season the fish, and within just a couple of minutes you have a meal fit for a king. This watercress butter, incidentally, is also great with a steak, pork or lamb chops, or roast chicken.

Serves 4 as a main course

15g (½oz) soft butter
4 x 175g (6oz) portions of hake, grey sea or red mullet, mackerel, turbot, brill or
    John Dory, skin on (scaled if necessary)
salt and freshly ground black pepper

FOR THE WATERCRESS BUTTER
75g (3oz) butter, softened
1 clove of garlic, peeled and crushed or finely grated
15g (½oz) chopped watercress (2 generous tbsp)
twist of black pepper
2 tsp lemon juice

Place a sheet of baking parchment on the work surface. Mix all the ingredients for the watercress butter together in a bowl. Form the butter into a sausage shape, then roll up in the paper. Place in the fridge to firm up (or if you need it straight away you can pop it into the freezer to chill). The butter will keep in the fridge for a week, or in the freezer for up to 3 months.

When you are ready to cook the fish, place a heavy cast-iron griddle pan or frying pan on a high heat and allow to get very hot. Spread the soft butter on the flesh side of the fish and season with salt and pepper. Place the fish in the hot pan (no extra butter or oil is needed), flesh side down, and cook for 2–4 minutes until golden underneath – the time will depend on the heat of the pan and the fish that you're using. Turn the fish over and cook for a further couple of minutes until just cooked through.

Place the fish on warm plates and top with a slice of the watercress butter, which will slowly melt over the fish. Serve with a green salad.

HALIBUT EN PAPILLOTE

En papillote, which literally means in 'parchment', is a nifty little method of cooking food in a parcel before baking it. Fish cooks beautifully when wrapped in a paper pouch, ensuring that none of the precious juices are lost in baking, and you also have the added advantage of being able to top it with anything from a slice of lemon and sprigs of herbs to a little salsa like this tomato and coriander one here.

Serves 4 as a main course

4 x 175g (6oz) thick fillets of halibut
salt and freshly ground black pepper
1 small lime, quartered, to serve

FOR THE SALSA
12 cherry tomatoes, quartered
4 spring onions, trimmed and chopped
1 clove of garlic, peeled and chopped
2 tbsp chopped coriander
1 tsp chopped chilli pepper (deseeded, if you wish)
3 tbsp extra virgin olive oil
1 tbsp lemon juice
good pinch of salt
good pinch of sugar
freshly ground black pepper

Preheat the oven to 200°C (400°F), Gas mark 6.

Cut four sheets of greaseproof paper big enough to fold over the fish to make a parcel. Place each piece of halibut on a sheet and sprinkle with salt and pepper.

Combine all the ingredients for the salsa then divide it evenly over the fish.

Seal up the parcels, place on a baking sheet and cook in the oven for about 15 minutes until the fish is just cooked through. Drizzle the juice of a lime quarter over each fish just before serving. Serve with some boiled potatoes and a green salad.

IRISH STEW WITH PEARL BARLEY

There's no point in trying to reinvent the wheel when it comes to our great national dish. Having said that, I do love sneaking in lots of gutsy garlic. For the best result, be sure to ask for thick chops on the bone. When made well it's not hard to see why this is one of Ireland's favourite dishes.

Serves 4–6 as a main course

4 x 350g (12oz), 3cm (1¼in) thick gigot lamb chops, with bone in
   (1.4kg/3lb 2oz total weight)
salt and freshly ground black pepper
250g (9oz) carrots (small carrots scrubbed and halved at an angle, or large
   carrots, peeled and cut at an angle into 4cm/1½in pieces)
250g (9oz) celery, trimmed and cut at an angle into 4cm (1½in) pieces
3 onions, peeled and each cut into 6 wedges
8 large cloves of garlic, peeled and left whole
50g (2oz) pearl barley
600ml (1 pint) lamb or chicken stock
8–12 potatoes
2 tbsp chopped parsley leaves

Preheat the oven to 170°C (325°F), Gas mark 3.

Place a flameproof casserole (or large saucepan) on a medium–high heat. Trim the excess fat from the chops and place the scraps of fat in the pan so that they can render. Meanwhile, cut the chops in half lengthways so as not to go through the bone. When some fat has melted into the pan, pick out the unmelted/unrendered bits (and eat them or give them to your dogs!), turn the heat up to high and place the chops in the pan. Cook on both sides, seasoning with salt and pepper, until brown, then transfer them to a plate.

Add the carrots, celery, onions and garlic to the pan, season with salt and pepper and toss on the heat for a couple of minutes until starting to go slightly golden at the edges. Return the meat (and all the juices) to the pan with the barley and stock and stir to combine. Bring to the boil, cover and cook in the oven for 1 hour.

Meanwhile, peel the potatoes and halve if large. Once the hour is up, take the pan out of the oven and place the potatoes on top. Cover and put back in the oven for 35–45 minutes until cooked. Scatter with parsley and serve from the pan.

POTATO AND SAGE GRATIN

This is the kind of comforting, creamy potato gratin I make over and over again. Change, or omit, the herb depending on what you're serving with this dish. Best made with a floury potato on a cold winter's day, it's divine with everything from a piece of pan-fried fish to a hearty beef casserole.

Serves 4–6 as a side dish

75g (3oz) butter
3 cloves of garlic, peeled and crushed or finely grated
2 tbsp sliced sage leaves
300ml (11fl oz) double or regular cream
½ nutmeg, grated, or ½ tsp ground nutmeg
salt and freshly ground black pepper
800g (1¾lb) peeled potatoes (about 1kg/2lb 2oz before peeling), cut into 1cm
　　(½in) slices

Preheat the oven to 180°C (350°F), Gas mark 4.

Rub a 1 litre (1¾ pint) pie dish with a little of the butter and set aside.

Place the rest of the butter in a pan, put on a high heat and allow to foam – don't let it burn. Add the garlic and sage and cook until the garlic is just turning a pale gold. Do not let it brown. Add the cream, then the nutmeg and a good pinch of salt and pepper. Bring to a bubble, then set aside.

Sprinkle some salt and pepper in the pie dish and arrange a layer of potato slices in the bottom, then add a little more seasoning and another layer of potato and continue layering until all the potato is in. Pour the contents of the pan over the potatoes, making sure the garlic and sage are evenly distributed. Cover with foil and bake for 20–30 minutes, then uncover and bake for a further 30–40 minutes until the potatoes are completely tender in the centre and golden. Serve.

POTATO AND ROSEMARY SODA FOCACCIA

This is an Irish version of an Italian classic, but using some of our very best produce: wheat, spuds and dairy – what could be better?

The trick to getting a great soda dough is minimal handling. As soon as it comes together, take your hand out, shape the bread and get it into the oven as soon as possible. And don't forget to be generous with the olive oil!

Makes 1 focaccia

250g (9oz) potatoes, scrubbed, skins left on, cut into 3mm- (1/8in-) thick slices
6 tbsp extra virgin olive oil, plus extra for drizzling
2 sprigs of fresh rosemary, leaves pulled off the stalks
2 tsp salt
good twist of black pepper
450g (1lb) plain flour, plus extra for dusting
1 level kitchen tsp* bread soda or bicarbonate of soda
400ml (14fl oz) buttermilk
75g (3oz) finely grated cheese, such as Cheddar or Gruyère

Preheat the oven to 230°C (450°F), Gas mark 8. Place a large saucepan of water on to boil. When it boils, add the potato slices, then bring back up to the boil on a high heat. Boil the potatoes for just 1 minute, then drain carefully, so as not to break them up. Place the potatoes in a large bowl or on a tray and drizzle with 4 tablespoons of the olive oil and scatter over the rosemary, 1 teaspoon of the and the pepper. Mix gently, then set aside.

Now make the bread dough. Sift the flour, remaining salt and soda into a bowl, then make a well in the centre and pour in all the buttermilk. Using your hand outstretched to look like a claw, go around the sides of the bowl to bring the flour and liquid together. Don't knead it or it will be tough. Stop mixing once it all comes together.

Oil a baking tray, or a large Swiss roll tin, with the remaining olive oil and lightly flour the worktop. Pat or roll out the dough on the worktop to a piece larger than an A4 sheet of paper. Transfer to the prepared tray and arrange the potatoes, rosemary and oil on top. Sprinkle with the cheese and bake for 25–35 minutes until golden and cooked in the centre.

Take out of the oven, then drizzle with a little more olive oil and allow to sit on the baking tray for 10 minutes. Transfer to a wire rack and leave to cool completely.

* Always ensure you accurately measure out your bread soda using measuring spoons

HONEY AND ALMOND CAKE

A deliciously simple cake with sweet, fragrant honey and nutty, moist ground almonds. All it needs is a cup of tea or coffee on the side.

Serves 6–8

150g (5oz) unsalted butter, plus extra for greasing
150g (5oz) honey
50g (2oz) icing sugar
4 eggs
1 tsp vanilla extract
225g (8oz) ground almonds
75g (3oz) whole almonds (with skins on), cut lengthways into 2–3 slices

FOR THE ICING
150g (5oz) icing sugar
1½–2 tbsp lemon juice

Preheat the oven to 170°C (325°F), Gas mark 3. Line the base of a round 23cm (9in) spring-form cake tin with baking paper and grease the sides with butter.

Place the butter in a saucepan on the heat and melt, then set aside. Put 100g (3½oz) of the honey, the icing sugar, eggs and vanilla extract into a bowl and, using an electric whisk, beat for 3–4 minutes until light and fluffy and slightly paler in colour. Add the melted butter and ground almonds and mix well to combine.

Pour into the prepared tin and bake in the oven for 25–30 minutes until a skewer inserted into the centre of the cake comes out clean. Once cooked, take the cake out of the oven and allow it to stand for 5 minutes. Leave the oven on.

Place the sliced almonds on a tray and cook in the oven for 6–8 minutes until light golden, then take out and cool. Meanwhile, place the remaining honey in a small saucepan and allow it to get hot.

To remove the cake from the tin, run a small sharp knife around the side of the cake, then carefully unclip the sides of the tin and remove. Take a plate, but not your serving plate, tip the cake over onto it and remove the base of the tin and the sheet of paper. Then take your cake serving plate, put it over the cake and flip it over. While the cake is still hot, pour the hot honey over the top, then allow it to cool completely.

To make the icing, mix the icing sugar with enough lemon juice to make a spreadable icing. Using a palette knife or the back of a spoon (dipped in boiling water for help if you need it), spread the icing over the top of the cake, then scatter the toasted almonds over the top. Allow the cake to sit for 10–15 minutes for the icing to set.

HOW TO MAKE A HOT WHISKEY

Each publican in Ireland will have a strong opinion on which Irish whiskey makes the best hot whiskey – Paddy or Powers? Either way, here's the standard recipe that fixes everything from a cough and cold to a mild case of heartache.

Serves 1

1 measure (35.5ml/generous 1¼fl oz) of Irish whiskey
1 generous tsp brown sugar
5 cloves
1 slice of lemon
150ml (4fl oz) boiling water

Put the whiskey and sugar into a heatproof glass. Stick the cloves into the lemon slice and place in the glass. Pour in the boiling water and stir to dissolve the sugar. Serve.

I've always loved Dingle. It's hard not to: this bustling port epitomises everything great about traditional Irish towns, from the pubs that double as shops to the creative atmosphere that permeates virtually every cobble and stone in the place.

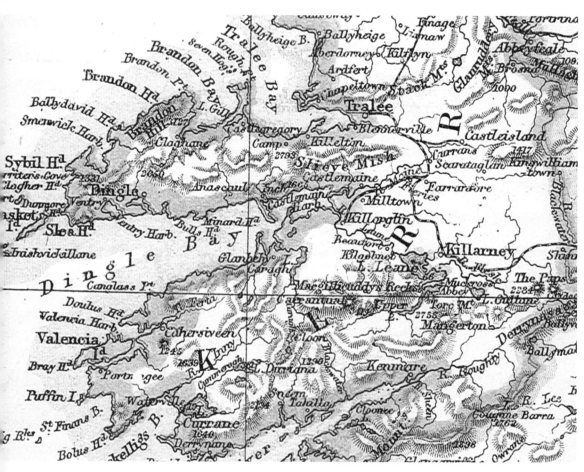

THE DINGLE

PENINSULA

THE DINGLE PENINSULA

After a marvellous day on the Ring of Kerry, I hit the road on a new day, comforted in the knowledge that there's plenty of fine scenery to come. My destination today is the *other* peninsular drive in Kerry, centred on the bustling and popular port town of Dingle.

I head north toward Castlemaine and then veer west onto a road that's narrow enough – I once was stuck on it for two hours because of a broken-down tractor up ahead, but Dingle is worth every effort to get there. After about 20km (and no traffic obstructions) I reach Inch, on the water's edge. It is an often deserted expanse of sand, beautifully secluded, which is a favourite for surfers. You might recognise the 5km-long beach from the movies: it had a starring role in David Lean's 1970 epic love story, *Ryan's Daughter*.

I turn inland and pass Anasacaul, which is famous for Tom Crean's South Pole Inn, which the explorer ran after his exploits in the Antarctic alongside Robert Scott and Ernest Shackleton made him a legend. I continue on my way, though, and soon I'm in Dingle … and the heart of the action.

I've always loved Dingle. It's hard not to: this bustling port epitomises everything great about traditional Irish towns, from the pubs that double as shops to the creative atmosphere that permeates virtually every cobble and stone in the place. This is a great centre for music, for visual arts and, invariably, for food, with plenty of local growers and farmers earning kudos for their excellent produce.

A fine example is Jerry Kennedy's butcher's shop, a family-run place that has been a Dingle fixture for generations because of the extraordinary quality of its cuts and its emphasis on in-house products like Blasket Island lamb – which is only in season in late summer and autumn. The meat is beautiful, and needs little to complement its sweet flavour. The quality of the meat is perfect for roasting, and thinking about their lamb sends me to the kitchen later to cook Ballymaloe roast rack of lamb (see page 147), dressed only with a fresh and simple mint and apple chutney.

Dingle is also home to some excellent brewers and distillers. Just north-east of the centre is the Dingle Brewing Company, which was founded in 2011 and has made a big splash with its creamy Crean's Lager, named after the explorer and available all over town. Not far away is the Dingle Whiskey Distillery, an artisan factory that makes not just its own whiskey, but a quintuple-distilled vodka and even its own gin (it's only one of a few Irish companies to make it), which has all the elements of a traditional London dry gin but has a unique flavour due to its original choice of (secret) botanicals.

Dingle is also the birthplace of Murphy's, where two brothers inspired by artisan ice-cream makers in the United States came home and set about creating their own selection of Irish-influenced flavours. I'm torn between brown bread and sea salt, Guinness and Kilbeggan whiskey!

A great place for a bite is Out of the Blue, a shack-style restaurant down at the port, where you can eat with the waters lapping at the harbour walls and the scent of the ocean lingering in the air. This is the place to come for seafood and fish, spanking fresh from the sea and delivered to your plate. The menu changes daily, depending on the catch; if for some reason the catch isn't good enough, they just won't open. How's that for commitment to the very best of fresh produce?

I can barely tear myself away from the charms of the town, but my reward is the Slea Head drive. Only 50km long, this circular route around the tip of the peninsula is one of Ireland's best scenic drives, and I could easily spend a whole day exploring every beach, ancient beehive hut and Iron Age fort I encounter along the way.

About 7km southwest of Ventry I stop at one such fort, the Dunbeg Fort Visitor Centre, which has a beehive hut and also a terrific little café called the Stonehouse that serves a fine crab sandwich, making the most of local seafood.

At Dunquin I stop again and look out to sea at the foreboding Blasket Island, blanketed by waves and wind and populated until 1953, when the last of the islanders finally gave up their hardscrabble life and migrated to the mainland. It's a 20-minute boat ride to the Great Blasket in clement conditions, but when you arrive on the deserted island, peppered with the crumbling homes of its long-since gone inhabitants, it's like stepping back in time at least 100 years.

At Clogher I stop again, this time to visit Louis Mulcahy's pottery shop where each piece is made in the local workshop. Upstairs, the Caifé na Caolóige follows the same theme: everything is homemade and the Mulcahys are devoted to supporting local producers, so the cheese– Dilliskus, Kilcummin and Fenugreek – comes from Maja Binder's Dingle Peninsula Cheese farm just outside Castlegregory, on the north side of the peninsula. The brown bread is made in Ventry and the eggs are hatched in Lispole, halfway between Anascaul and Dingle on the N86. In fact, Maja's partner Olivier Beaujean is a former chef and pork butcher who has turned his skills to foraging: his specialty is home-smoked fish flavoured with seaweed (which I also find in Maja's Dilliskus cheese). He also does a fine line in pickled sea vegetables. The flavours of the Dillisk stay with me, and when I return I use this to make White soda bread with Dillisk – a tasty and healthy bread inspired by this delicious sea vegetable from Ireland's west coast (see page 155).

All of this food needs something to wash it down with, and I can't think of anything better than a bottle of Carraig Dubh, a hand-crafted traditional porter from the West Kerry Brewery, about a mile outside the village of Ballyferriter. There aren't a lot of women involved in craft brewing in Ireland, so I'm secretly pleased to see that the brewer here is Adrienne Heslin, who along with Paul O'Loingsigh uses fresh well water to create wonderful dark beers.

I return to Dingle in a state of foodie elation. I'm ready to settle in for the night, and what better spot than the family-run Heaton's Guesthouse. Seeing as Dingle is one of the busiest towns in Ireland, you might need a second option! Another great place is John and Mary Curran's Greenmount House, surely one of Ireland's finest guesthouses. The Irish B&B tradition is very much alive and well here: the rooms are wonderfully comfortable, the breakfast is perfect and the views are to die for. No wonder they travel from all over the world just to be in this corner of Kerry.

PAN-STEAMED HAKE WITH DILLISK CREAM SAUCE

The wonderfully salty dillisk seaweed works a treat in this rich creamy sauce, which can be paired with any round fish.

Serves 4 as a main course

25g (1oz) butter
60g (2½oz) shallots, peeled and finely chopped
2 tsp finely chopped dried dillisk seaweed (dulse)
100ml (3½fl oz) double or regular cream
75g (3oz) butter, cut into cubes
4 x 185g (6½oz) fillets of hake, grey sea mullet or bass, scaled
salt and freshly ground black pepper

Put the butter, shallots and dillisk in a saucepan, cover with a lid and sweat gently on a low heat for 5–7 minutes until softened.

When soft, add the cream and cook, uncovered, until the mixture has reduced by half. Take off the heat and set aside for a couple of minutes to cool down to tepid. Place back on a low heat and whisk in the butter, lump by lump. Add a tiny dash of water if it is very thick.

Pour 100ml (3½fl oz) water into a pan that will fit all the fish together in a single layer. Add the fish, skin side down, season with salt and pepper and cover with a lid. Place the pan on a low heat and allow to bubble and steam gently. The fish will take about 10 minutes to cook through.

Thin out the cream sauce to a light coating consistency with 4–5 tablespoons of the water from the fish pan (bulk up with hot water if necessary). Divide the fish among four plates and spoon some of the sauce over each fillet. Serve with boiled potatoes and a leafy green salad.

RACHEL'S TIP
This sauce can be made ahead and kept warm like the beurre blanc on page 104.

BALLYMALOE ROAST RACK OF LAMB WITH FRESH APPLE AND MINT CHUTNEY

A rack is a deliciously tender cut of lamb that, once it's been prepared, is easy to carve and serve. Ask your butcher to prepare it for roasting if you'd rather not do it yourself.

The apple and mint chutney is particularly good with young sweet lamb in the spring or summer.

Serves 4–6 as a main course

2 racks of spring lamb (6–8 cutlets each)
salt and freshly ground black pepper

FOR THE FRESH APPLE AND MINT CHUTNEY
1 large cooking apple (such as Grenadier or Bramley Seedling), peeled and cored
large handful of fresh mint leaves – Spearmint or Bowles mint
50g (2oz) onions, peeled and roughly chopped
20–50g (¾–2oz) caster sugar (depending on tartness of apple)
salt and cayenne pepper, to season

Preheat the oven to 220°C (425°F), Gas mark 7.

Score the fat of the racks into roughly 2–3cm (¾–1¼in) squares or diamonds, making sure to cut through only the fat, not the meat. Sprinkle the scored fat with salt and pepper and place on a roasting tray, fat side up. You can either cook it straight away or refrigerate until needed.

Roast the racks for 25–35 minutes depending on the age of the lamb (very small racks in spring might take just 25 minutes, but larger racks later on in the year might take 35 minutes to cook) and degree of doneness required. When cooked, remove the lamb to a warm serving dish. Turn off the oven and leave the lamb to rest for 5–10 minutes before carving.

Meanwhile, put the apple, mint, onions and sugar in a food processor and whiz to combine, then season with salt and cayenne pepper.

Carve the lamb and serve 2–3 cutlets per person, depending on the size of the cutlets. Serve with the chutney.

PORK AND CORIANDER STEW

A big hearty dish with gorgeous Moorish flavours, this will not mind at all being cooked a day or two in advance and gently reheated.

Serves 6–8 as a main course

3 tbsp coriander seeds
1.5kg (3¼lb) prepared neck of pork (i.e. off the bone, skin and excess fat removed), cut into 2–4cm (¾–1½in) cubes
1 tsp black peppercorns, cracked
1 tsp salt
4 cloves of garlic, peeled and bashed but not completely crushed
500ml (18fl oz) red wine
3 tbsp extra virgin olive oil
3 large red onions, each peeled and cut into 10 wedges
50g (2oz) chopped coriander, leaves and stalks
1 tbsp sherry vinegar

Toast the coriander seeds in a dry non-stick pan on a medium–high heat for a minute or so, tossing once or twice, until slightly darker in colour and toasted. Tip the toasted seeds into a mortar and crush with a pestle until coarse, or allow to cool, then place in a plastic bag and crush with a rolling pin.

Place the pork in a bowl, add the crushed coriander, black peppercorns, salt, garlic and wine and leave to marinate overnight.

Next day, preheat the oven to 170°C (325°F), Gas mark 3. Place a flameproof casserole or large saucepan on a medium–high heat. Add 2 tablespoons of the olive oil and allow to get hot, then pick the pork out of the marinade (save the marinade) and brown in three batches in the pot. Set each batch aside while you brown the next. Once it is all browned, add the remaining olive oil, toss in the red onions and season with salt and pepper. Cook the onions for 1–2 minutes, then tip in all the meat and the marinade and bring up to a simmer. Cover and transfer to the oven, then cook for 1½–2 hours until tender.

Stir in the chopped coriander and sherry vinegar and serve with a green salad and the cooked butter beans and seasonal greens.

PORK SCHNITZEL WITH SAGE BUTTER

A pork version of the traditional German veal schnitzel, this is a great family favourite in our house. Feel free to ring the changes with the flavoured butter, or use other greens such as wild garlic, watercress or parsley. Chicken, turkey, beef and lamb also work well.

Serves 4–6 as a main course

600–700g (1lb 6oz–1lb 8oz) fillet of pork, cut at an angle into 1cm- (½in-) thick slices
50g (2oz) plain flour
salt and freshly ground black pepper
100g (3½oz) fine white breadcrumbs (fresh or frozen)
grated zest of ½ lemon
2 eggs, beaten
butter and extra virgin olive oil, for frying

FOR THE SAGE BUTTER
2 cloves of garlic, peeled and crushed
100g (3½oz) soft butter
1 tbsp chopped sage
1 tbsp lemon juice

Mix all the ingredients for the sage butter in a bowl. Put on a sheet of greaseproof paper, roll into a log and chill.

Place the pork fillet slices between two sheets of cling film and, using a rolling pin, gently beat until flattened to about 5mm (¼in) thick.

Mix the flour with a pinch of salt and a twist of pepper in a bowl big enough to toss the pork in; in another bowl mix the breadcrumbs with ¼ teaspoon of salt, a few twists of pepper and the lemon zest; and in a third bowl whisk the eggs together. Dip each piece of pork into the flour, then into the egg and then in the crumbs. Make sure they are well coated.

Heat 1 tablespoon each of butter and olive oil in a frying pan and fry the schnitzels in batches, adding more butter and oil when needed. Keep the cooked schnitzels, uncovered, in a warm oven while you cook the rest.

Serve with slices of sage butter melting on top. Can be served with a salad and seasonal greens.

BUTTER-ROASTED CAULIFLOWER

I absolutely love how with roasted cauliflower you get a sweet nutty flavour that is altogether different from when it's boiled. Add ground spices such as cumin and coriander, if you wish.

Serves 4–6 as a side dish

1 head of cauliflower
50g (2oz) butter
salt and freshly ground black pepper

Preheat the oven to 230°C (450°F), Gas mark 8.

Remove the dark green leaves from the cauliflower and discard, then peel off the light green tender leaves and chop coarsely. Set aside.

Cut the cauliflower head into walnut-sized florets, with all the stems attached (don't discard these).

Melt the butter and pour into a large bowl. Add the cauliflower florets and toss with some salt and pepper.

Lay the cauliflower out in a single layer in a roasting tin and roast for 6 minutes. Take out the tin and turn the florets, then toss in the leaves and cook for a further 6 minutes or until golden and almost tender. Serve.

ROAST JERUSALEM ARTICHOKES

Roasting Jerusalem artichokes really brings out their flavour - simple and delicious!

Serves 4 as a side dish

500g (1lb 2oz) Jerusalem artichokes, scrubbed very well
4 tbsp extra virgin olive oil
sea salt and freshly ground black pepper

Preheat the oven to 200°C (400°F), Gas mark 6. Place a piece of baking parchment on a baking tray.

Cut the artichokes in half or even quarters if they're very large. Toss in a bowl with the olive oil and season with salt and pepper. Tip onto the tray and place in the oven.

Cook for 50–60 minutes, turning over once or twice during cooking. Be careful towards the end as they may burn, but do keep going until they are really golden and sticky. Serve immediately.

Serves about 6 as a side dish

900g (2lb) swede turnip
salt and lots of freshly ground black pepper
50–110g (2–3¾oz) butter

FOR THE CARAMELISED ONIONS
2–3 tbsp extra virgin olive oil
450g (1lb) onions, peeled, halved and thinly sliced

TO SERVE
1 tbsp chopped parsley leaves

Peel the turnip thickly to remove all the outside skin, then cut it into about 2cm (¾in) cubes. Put into a high-sided pan and cover with water, then add a good pinch of salt. Bring to the boil, then turn the heat down a little and cook until soft – this can take between 45–60 minutes.

Meanwhile, heat the olive oil in a heavy saucepan. Toss in the onions and cook on a low heat for 30–45 minutes, until they soften and caramelise to a rich golden brown, making sure to stir and scrape the bottom of the pan (I use a wooden spatula for this) every 5–10 minutes.

Drain the turnip, then mash well and beat in the butter. Taste and season with lots of pepper and more salt if necessary. Sprinkle with caramelised onions and chopped parsley to serve.

SWEDE TURNIP WITH CARAMELISED ONIONS

Swede turnips are stronger in flavour than the little white turnips. They are picked only after a couple of frosts have occurred, as this is when they turn deliciously sweet. The caramelised onions, with their luscious richness, add another dimension to the dish. We make this at Ballymaloe. It's wonderful served with a big hearty stew or a Sunday roast.

WHITE SODA BREAD WITH DILLISK

Teeming with goodness, seaweed has been at the top of the healthy foods list for many a century, and in Ireland, while every single seaweed is edible, some are more palatable than others. Dillisk, otherwise known as dulse, one of the most popular, is a red algae that can range in colour from bright reddish-purple to dull reddish-brown. Often dried and eaten as a snack on Ireland's west and north coasts, this sea vegetable, which is bursting with iron, potassium, zinc and calcium, works a treat in a simple soda bread that just cries out for a nice slathering of good Irish butter.

Makes 1 loaf

10g (scant ½oz) dried dillisk seaweed (dulse)
450g (1lb) plain flour, plus extra for dusting
1 tsp salt
1 level kitchen tsp* bread soda or bicarbonate of soda
400ml (14fl oz) buttermilk

Preheat the oven to 230°C (450°F), Gas mark 8.

Break the seaweed into pieces, then put on a baking tray and cook in the oven for 2 minutes or until just crisp. Take out of the oven (leave the oven on) and break the seaweed up into little pieces. Sometimes I find that the seaweed gets quite tough – if this is the case then you can put it with some of the flour (about a handful) into a food processor and whiz to chop up the seaweed.

Lightly flour a baking tray and the worktop. Place the seaweed and flour in a large bowl, add the salt and sift in the bread soda (make sure to sift it or you could end up with yellow/green spots in your bread). Stir to combine the dry ingredients, then, using your hand, make a well in the centre and pour in all the buttermilk. Using your hand outstretched to look like a claw, go around the sides of the bowl to bring the flour and liquid together. Don't knead it or it will be tough. Once the mixture has come together, form it into a round on the worktop and flour the top, then turn it over once (but do not knead) and make a round about 2.5cm (1in) high and 18cm (7in) in diameter. Place on the floured tray, flour the blade of a knife and cut a cross in the loaf.

Place in the oven and cook for 10 minutes, then turn the oven temperature down to 200°C (400°F), Gas mark 6 and cook for a further 25–35 minutes until the base sounds hollow when tapped. Take out and cool on a wire rack.

*Always ensure you accurately measure out your bread soda using measuring spoons

GRILLED PLUMS WITH WHISKEY AND CLOTTED CREAM

A super-fast recipe that transforms a few plums into a great dinner party dessert. Use softly whipped cream or vanilla ice cream if you can't get clotted cream.

Serves 2–4

4 ripe plums, halved and pitted
2 tbsp Irish whiskey (optional)
2–4 tbsp soft light brown sugar
clotted cream, to serve

Preheat the grill.

Place the plum halves, cut side up, in a gratin dish and drizzle with the whiskey (if using), then scatter the sugar over.

Place under the grill and cook for 7–10 minutes until the plums are juicy and bubbling and the sugar has caramelised. Serve with clotted cream.

The road to Limerick City takes me past Tralee and then Adare, described as the prettiest village in Ireland. It's a beautiful place, lined with brightly coloured thatched cottages.

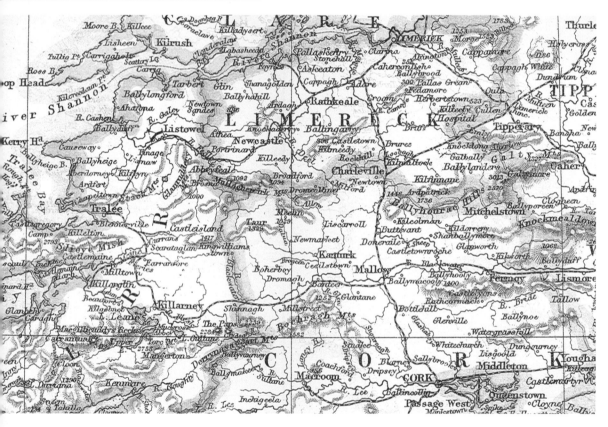

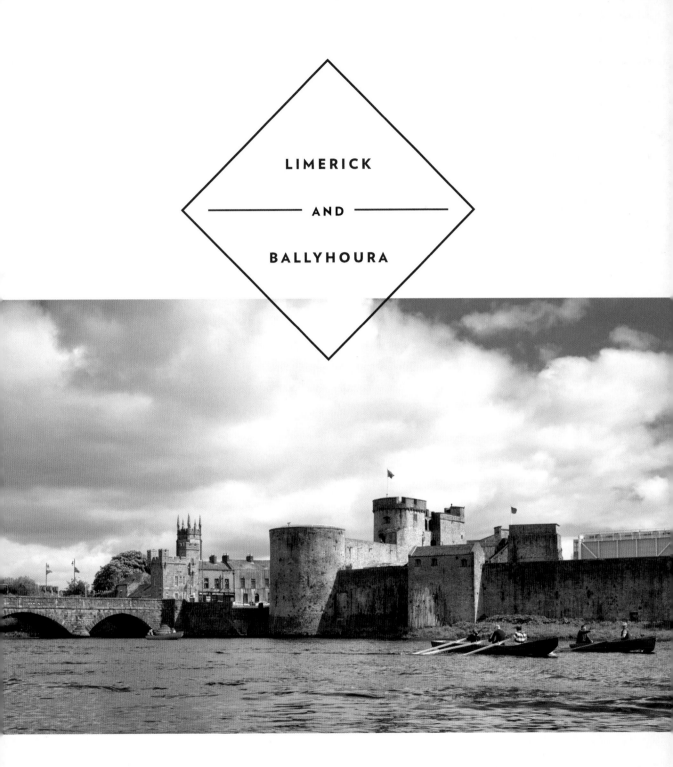

LIMERICK

AND

BALLYHOURA

LIMERICK AND BALLYHOURA

Not long after departing Dingle, I come across another stunning scenic drive, this time through the Connor Pass, Ireland's highest mountain at 456m. It's a beautiful day, so the views of Dingle and its harbour to the south and mighty Mount Brandon to the north are breathtaking.

The road to Limerick City takes me past busy Tralee and as far as Adare, which is regularly described as the prettiest village in Ireland. It's a beautiful place, lined with brightly coloured thatched cottages occupied by a wide variety of craft shops and cafés.

Occupying another thatched cottage on Main Street is the excellent Restaurant 1826 Adare, where chef Wade Murphy and his wife Elaine keep one of the best restaurants in Munster ticking over with superb service and a delicious menu made up of locally sourced ingredients transformed into exquisite cuisine. Here all the meat is pasture reared, the fish is sustainably sourced and the cheeses made by local artisan cheese-makers. With signature dishes such as warm chicken liver salad with piccalilli, pickles and Bally greens and Head to Tail Free Range Pork Tasting Plate, it is no wonder that this restaurant has won so many awards. And, just to prove that Adare knows a thing or two about high-quality hospitality, on the northern edge of town is one of the grandest hotels in all of Ireland, Adare Manor, a gorgeous estate that is also home to one of the best parkland golf courses in the country.

DETOUR: THE MUSTARD SEED AT ECHO LODGE

About a 20-minute drive south of Adare, in the lovely village of Ballingarry, is one of the finest restaurants in the country. Dan Mullane's Mustard Seed offers a four-course seasonal menu which is carefully created with locally sourced produce, including vegetables and fruits grown in the 7-acre gardens that surround this former 19th-century convent. There is something for everyone on the menu, from fish and seafood to lamb, beef and duck, and not forgetting the vegetarian diners, too. If you're in no mood to move after the exquisite dinner (which is highly likely!), the elegant country-style rooms are definitely worth considering.

I'm on the road again, destination Limerick City. There's so much to see and do in the city that in 2014 was chosen as Ireland's City of Culture, from the Limerick City Gallery of Art to the excellent Hunt Museum, home to 2,000-odd treasures from the Bronze Age to the Middle Ages.

It's the weekend when I visit this city and the streets are filled with people enjoying their weekends, and many heading to the market. I am one of them; my first stop when I come here is always at the The Milk Market, one of the finest farmers' markets in the country. Local producers from all over the region gather to sell their marvellous wares: I can buy sausages, chutneys, cheeses, Ballyhoura mushrooms (some of my favourites – I use these in my Venison and red wine stew, see page 268) seaweeds and juices from a host of Irish producers, but plenty more besides – there are vintage clothing stalls, a crêperie, bakers and horticulturalists selling everything from seeds to bouquets of wildflowers. One of my favourite stalls is Silver Darlings, which specialises in pickled herring with different herbs and spices – it reminds me of my childhood visits to my mother's home in Iceland. Spices are a great match for pickled or raw fish – I use cumin in my Carpaccio of fish with blood orange and cumin (see page 164). You could easily spend a whole day just wandering from stall to stall, soaking up the atmosphere, inspired by the aromas and the colours that pack the streets.

Another great spot for quality food in a great atmosphere is Cornstore at Home, which focuses on quality food locally sourced. If you'd like someone to do the cooking for you, you can go upstairs to the restaurant or pop into the always

elegant French Table, which offers fine French dining but is a lovely spot for a tasty and informal lunch too.

My place of choice to stay in the city is 1 Pery Square, a gorgeous boutique hotel. They serve such delicious food, I will certainly be back again!

DETOUR: BALLYHOURA COUNTRY

South of Limerick and stretching into north Cork is Ballyhoura Country, named after the small mountain range that runs from east to west for about 10km along the border between the two counties. In the last decade, enterprising businesses throughout the region pulled together and collaborated to give the area its own distinctive tourist identity. They did this through combining outdoor activities like hiking and mountain biking with traditional experiences such as crossroads dancing at the Ballinvreena Rambling House and road bowling along the country roads of north Cork. All these activities were included to give visitors a unique insight into how rural Ireland has adapted to contemporary times, but without giving up the things that make it so special. It works; here the Ireland of the past, present and future rub together harmoniously. And for the foodies like me, the reward after all this activity is visiting one of the lovely farmers' markets in the area – in particular the one every Monday in Kilmallock.

South of Kilmallock I cross the border into north Cork: I want to visit the Eight Degrees Brewery, just outside Mitchelstown. This is artisanal brewing at its best, and I have the choice of five delicious brews: Barefoot Bohemian Pilsner Lager, Howling Gale Irish Pale Ale, Sunburnt Irish Red Ale, Knockmealdown Irish Stout and Amber Ella American Ale, which was a 2014 World Beer Cup medal winner. I have some driving yet to do, so I pick up one of each and put it aside – a nice beer at day's end is a just reward. Some of the beer even makes it home with me at the end of my trip, and makes a delicious and decadent addition to Lamb shanks braised in red ale (see page 181).

After exploring Limerick City I'm back on the road again, heading northwest past the folk park at Bunratty and Shannon Airport … all the way to Newmarket-on-Fergus, just over the border into County Clare. Just north of town is the ancestral pile of the O'Brien family, Dromoland Castle, now one of the grandest hotels in the country. Its crenallated towers greet me from afar, the welcoming lights glowing from inside the ancient stone walls. Wonderful rooms, wonderful restaurant: satisfied and tired, I go to bed excited about my next destination: exploring County Clare and the Burren.

CARPACCIO OF FISH WITH BLOOD ORANGE AND CUMIN

There's something about this starter that I absolutely adore. The warm nutty flavour of the cumin works perfectly with the tangy orange juices over the delicately succulent slices of fish. This tastes like a warm sunny day somewhere very exotic.

Serves 4 as a starter

200g (7oz) very fresh fish fillet (such as cod or pollock), cut into 3cm- (1¼in-) slices
4 pinches of sea salt flakes
3 tbsp extra virgin olive oil
3 tsp lemon juice
1 tsp cumin seeds, toasted and ground (see page 149)
2 blood oranges, segmented (allow about 5 segments per plate) (see page 240)
1 handful of watercress sprigs (allow about 5 sprigs per plate)

Lay out the fish slices in a single layer on the plates and sprinkle with the sea salt flakes.

Mix the olive oil with the lemon juice, cumin and a small pinch of sea salt and drizzle over the fish.

Place the orange segments over the fish, gently squeezing them to sprinkle over a few drops of juice, and add the watercress sprigs. Serve.

RACHEL'S TIP
You can use mustard greens or rocket leaves if you like, in place of the watercress. Use regular oranges when out of season.

RED MULLET, SQUID AND COCKLE BOUILLABAISSE WITH AIOLI

I love a really great fish stew and this recipe takes a lot of inspiration from the traditional Provençal bouillabaisse, but with the added extras of smoked paprika and tomato aioli croutons. Of course, this recipe will welcome any other fish or shellfish in place of the red mullet, squid and cockles.

Serves 4–6 as a main course

250g (9oz) prepared squid (head and intestines discarded), tubes sliced into rings, wings and tentacles cut into strips

1 x 500–600g (1lb 2oz–1lb 6oz) red mullet, gutted, cleaned, scaled and cut into 2cm (¾in) pieces

20–30 cockles or clams in their shells, well washed and scrubbed – discard any that are not tightly shut or don't close when tapped

FOR THE BROTH
2 tbsp olive oil
200g (7oz) onion, peeled and cut into 1cm (½in) dice
225g (8oz) fennel bulb, trimmed and cut into 1cm (½in) dice
1 red pepper, deseeded and cut into 1cm (½in) dice
1 clove of garlic, peeled and sliced
good big pinch of saffron threads
1 bay leaf
salt and freshly ground black pepper
2 strips of orange rind
150ml (5fl oz) white wine
2 star anise
1 x 400g tin of chopped tomatoes
1 tsp sugar
700ml (1 pint 3fl oz) fish stock

FOR THE CROUTONS
4 thick slices of bread, cut into 2cm (¾in) chunks
4 tbsp olive oil

Continued overleaf.

RED MULLET, SQUID AND COCKLE
BOUILLABAISSE WITH AIOLI *Continued*

FOR THE MAYO

1 large egg yolk

2 tsp red wine vinegar

1 tsp tomato purée

1 tsp Dijon mustard

1 clove of garlic, peeled and crushed

good pinch of sugar

1 tbsp chopped coriander

1 tbsp chopped spring onion

75ml (3fl oz) olive oil

75ml (3fl oz) sunflower oil

First, make the broth. Heat the olive oil in a saucepan. Add the onion, fennel, red pepper, garlic, saffron and bay leaf with a good pinch of salt and pepper. Cover the pan and cook gently for 8–10 minutes until the vegetables are tender but not coloured. Add the orange rind, wine and star anise, uncover the pan and cook for a further 5 minutes. Add the tomatoes, 1 teaspoon of salt, the sugar, fish stock and squid, bring to the boil and cook for a further 5 minutes. Remove from the heat.

Next, make the croutons. Preheat the oven to 230°C (450°F), Gas mark 8. Drizzle the olive oil over the bread chunks and add a good sprinkling of salt and pepper. Put on a baking tray and bake for 6–8 minutes, until crisp.

Meanwhile, put all the ingredients for the aioli except the oils into a bowl and add a good pinch of salt and a good twist of pepper. Combine the oils in a jug and slowly drizzle into the bowl in a very thin stream, whisking all the time, until the mayo reaches a thick consistency.

Just before you want to serve, add the red mullet and cockles or clams to the broth, cover the pan and cook for a further 3 minutes. Discard any cockles or clams that remain closed. Ladle the bouillabaisse into bowls, spoon some aioli over the top and add the croutons. Serve.

CHICKEN CONFIT

Of course, duck is the bird that's best known for cooking in this style – slow simmering in rich fat on a gentle heat with some garlic and herbs. But other poultry and game also work well, such as pheasant, guinea fowl, rabbit and chicken. This is a wonderful way of both cooking the meat and preserving it too. Although it can be eaten straight away, it will keep in the fridge, in a bowl or pot, covered with the fat, for up to six months. I've included a few different ways to enjoy chicken confit, as I simply could not decide which recipe to include and which ones not to! When you've gone to the trouble of making a chicken confit it's great to have a few ways to use it.

Serves 4 as a main course

4 whole small chicken legs, or 4 large chicken drumsticks or thighs (about 1kg/2lb 2oz total weight)
325g (11½oz) duck or goose fat, or extra virgin olive oil
1 bay leaf
2 sprigs of fresh thyme
3 cloves of garlic, unpeeled and bashed
8 black peppercorns

FOR THE MARINADE
2 large sprigs of fresh thyme
2 bay leaves
1 tbsp sea salt
2 cloves of garlic, peeled and bashed
1 tsp cracked black peppercorns

Combine all the ingredients for the marinade, rub into the chicken and marinate overnight.

The next day, preheat the oven to 170°C (325°F), Gas mark 3.

Rinse the marinade off the chicken with cold water, then pat dry with kitchen paper, making sure to dry it very well.

Place the duck or goose fat or olive oil in an ovenproof saucepan that the chicken will fit snugly into. Add the bay leaf, thyme sprigs, garlic and black peppercorns.

Bring up to a simmer on the hob, adding more fat or olive oil if the chicken is not covered in it, then cover with a lid and transfer to the oven. Cook for 1–1½ hours until completely cooked, and the meat is almost falling off the bone, but not quite.

Pour into a deep bowl and ensure that the chicken is completely covered with the fat. Allow to cool, then cover and store in the fridge – it will keep for up to 6 months.

If using straight away, remove the chicken from the fat. Place a frying pan on a medium–high heat, add 1 tablespoon of the fat and place, skin side down, in the pan. Cook for 6–8 minutes till golden and crisp. If it has been in the fridge, preheat the oven to 200°C (400°F), Gas mark 6. Fry the chicken in the pan as above, then turn it over and pop it into the oven for a further 10–15 minutes to finish heating, before serving.

ROAST CHICKEN CONFIT WITH POTATOES, ONIONS AND LEEKS

A deliciously comforting dish that, once the chicken confit is made, takes just minutes to prepare and get on the table. For the best flavour, make sure to brown the chicken skin well.

Serves 4 as a main course

3 red onions, peeled and each cut into 6 wedges
2 medium leeks, trimmed, washed and cut at an angle into 2cm (¾in) pieces
4 potatoes, peeled and cut into 2cm (¾in) pieces
6 sprigs of fresh thyme
60ml (2½fl oz) chicken fat (from the chicken confit), or extra virgin olive oil
salt and freshly ground black pepper
4 chicken confit legs, thighs or drumsticks (see pages 170–171)

Preheat the oven to 220°C (425°F), Gas mark 7.

Place the onions, leeks, potatoes and thyme in a bowl. Mix in the chicken fat or olive oil and season with salt and pepper. Tip into a roasting tin and cook in the oven for 20–30 minutes until light golden and almost cooked – the potatoes should be nearly tender.

Meanwhile, place a large frying pan on a high heat and allow to get hot. Take the confit chicken out of the fat in the jar or bowl (if they have been sitting in the fridge) or out of the saucepan (if they have just been cooking in the pot) and place, skin side down, in the pan (there should be enough fat clinging to the legs to cook them in). Cook for 4–5 minutes until the skin is golden.

Take the potatoes, onions and leeks out of the oven, place the chicken, skin side up, on top of the vegetables and cook for a further 10 minutes. Take out of the oven when the chicken is hot through and the vegetables are tender.

CHICKEN CONFIT CASSOULET WITH CHORIZO CRUMBS

This is a twist on the classic cassoulet, which dates back as far as the early 1300s in the Languedoc region of France and gets its name from the earthenware casserole pot in which it's cooked. It's basically a stew of meat and haricot beans, but basic it is not. Often containing a variety of different meats, such as duck, goose, pork and mutton, a true cassoulet should be cooked long and slow to give a rich, yielding and succulent result.

Serves 4 as a main course

2 tbsp chicken, duck or goose fat, or extra virgin olive oil

2 sticks of celery, trimmed and finely chopped

150g (5oz) carrots (4 small carrots), peeled and finely chopped

200g (7oz) onions (2 small onions), peeled and finely chopped

2 cloves of garlic, peeled and chopped

salt and freshly ground black pepper

100g (3½oz) bacon lardons (0.5 x 2cm/¼ x ¾in), smoked or unsmoked

1 x 400g tin of chopped tomatoes

1 tsp sugar

475g (1lb 1oz) cooked haricot beans (or 240g/8½oz dried beans, soaked overnight and cooked, see page 111, and drained), or 2 x 400g tins, drained and rinsed

400ml (14fl oz) chicken stock

4 confit chicken legs, drumsticks or thighs (see pages 170–171)

FOR THE CHORIZO CRUMBS

3 tbsp extra virgin olive oil

60g (2½oz) chorizo, peeled if cured (soft, fresh chorizo doesn't need peeling) and finely chopped

60g (2½oz) fresh white breadcrumbs (or you can use frozen)

Place a medium–large saucepan or flameproof casserole on a medium heat, add the fat from the chicken confit or the olive oil, then tip in the celery, carrot, onion and garlic. Season with salt and pepper, turn down the heat, cover the pan and cook for 7–8 minutes till softened. Add the bacon lardons, cover again and cook for a further 5 minutes. Add the tomatoes, sugar, beans and stock and bring to the boil, then turn the heat down and simmer, uncovered, for 10–15 minutes until all the flavours have infused. Season to taste.

Meanwhile, place a frying pan on the heat and allow to get hot. Place the chicken pieces, with some fat clinging to them, skin side down in the pan and cook for about 5 minutes until golden. Then place, skin side up, in the pan with the tomato bean mixture and simmer for a further 10 minutes or until the chicken is hot in the centre. The cassoulet can be prepared ahead up to this point.

To make the chorizo crumbs, place a frying pan on a low–medium heat and before it has a chance to get hot add the olive oil and chopped chorizo and cook slowly for a few minutes, stirring regularly until lots of lovely amber-coloured oil has rendered from the chorizo and the chorizo itself has turned a little crispy. Remove the chorizo from the pan, leaving all the oil behind, and set aside. Tip the breadcrumbs into the oil in the pan. Stirring very regularly, cook the crumbs for a few minutes until they too become golden and a little crisp. Tip the chorizo back in and mix together, then tip out of the pan onto kitchen paper and set aside until you want to use it.

When ready to eat, preheat the grill. If it's been prepared ahead, heat the casserole on a medium heat for a few minutes, then scatter the chorizo crumbs over the top and cook under the grill until hot and bubbling, 3–4 minutes. Serve from the pot on the table with some kale or buttered cabbage.

CHICKEN CONFIT AND ROCKET SALAD WITH BLOOD ORANGES

In this delicious salad recipe the tangy blood orange segments cut through any richness in the chicken confit and complement the fresh base of peppery rocket greens. This is one of my favourites.

Serves 4 as a starter or light lunch

2 small chicken confit legs, thighs or drumsticks (see pages 170–171)
2 cloves of garlic, peeled and crushed or finely grated
50g (2oz) coarse white breadcrumbs
75g (3oz) rocket leaves or watercress

FOR THE DRESSING
2 blood oranges (if not in season, use ordinary oranges)
2 tbsp extra virgin olive oil
salt and freshly ground black pepper
1 tbsp lemon juice
1 small clove of garlic, peeled and crushed or finely grated

Place a frying pan on a high heat. Take the chicken out of the fat (either in the saucepan if just cooked or from the jar if in the fridge) and place, skin side down, in the hot pan. Cook for 4 minutes or until golden brown, then cook the other side for a further 3–4 minutes until heated through. The chicken confit takes longer to heat through if it has been in the fridge, about 15 minutes.

Remove the chicken from the pan, leaving 2 tablespoons or so of the fat in the pan, and place the pan back on the heat. Add the garlic and stir for a few seconds until very light golden, then tip in the breadcrumbs and stir on a medium–high heat until golden. Tip out onto a plate and set aside. When cool enough to handle, shred the chicken and cut the skin into strips.

Next, make the dressing. Segment the oranges (see page 240), then squeeze all the remaining juice out of the membrane and the peel into a small bowl. Add the olive oil, salt and pepper, lemon juice and garlic and stir to combine.

Place the rocket leaves or watercress in a bowl and dress with some or all of the dressing. Put the leaves on a large serving plate or individual plates. Arrange the orange segments and the torn chicken meat and skin over the leaves, then scatter the crumbs on top and serve.

LAMB SHANKS BRAISED IN RED ALE

I love how beer transforms in flavour when cooked. The gentle toasted malty twang of a red ale turns into something very mellow and deep when simmering away for a couple of hours with delicious meaty lamb shanks.

Serves 4 as a main course

4 lamb shanks
salt and freshly ground black pepper
400g (14oz) red onions, peeled and cut into wedges through the core
100g (3½oz) celery, trimmed and cut at an angle into 1cm (½in) chunks
8 cloves of garlic, peeled and sliced
2 tbsp chopped sage
250ml (9fl oz) red beer or ale
500ml (18fl oz) light lamb or chicken stock
1 tbsp tomato purée

Preheat the oven to 150°C (300°F), Gas mark 2.

Trim some fat from the shanks and render it on a medium heat in a pot big enough to take the four shanks. Season the shanks with salt and pepper.

Turn the heat up to high and fry the lamb shanks in the pot until golden on all sides. You might need to brown them two at a time. Remove the shanks, leaving any fat behind, then fry the onions, celery and garlic for a few minutes and season again.

Return the shanks to the pot with the sage, beer or ale, stock and tomato purée. Bring to the boil, then cover with a lid and cook in the oven for 2½–3 hours until the meat is succulent and almost falling off the bone.

Serve on a bed of roast garlic mash or plain mashed potatoes with plenty of the braising liquid.

QUICK FRESH GREEN SOUP

All cooks need in their repertoire a super-fast soup that can be whipped up in minutes. This particular soup is deliciously fresh in flavour, vibrant green in colour and, yes, it can be made from start to finish in 10 minutes. I normally use frozen peas for this.

Serves 4–6 as a starter

25g (1oz) butter
75g (3oz) spring onions, trimmed and chopped
salt and freshly ground black pepper
300g (11oz) cucumber, unpeeled, cut into 1cm (½in) dice
300g (11oz) frozen peas
750ml (1 pint 6fl oz) boiling chicken or vegetable stock
1 tbsp chopped mint
75ml (3fl oz) double or regular cream

Melt the butter in a saucepan on a medium heat and allow to foam. Add the spring onion and season with salt and pepper, then cook, uncovered, for 2–3 minutes. Add the cucumber, cover the pan and cook on a low heat for a few minutes until just softened. Add the peas and boiling stock, bring back to the boil and boil, uncovered, for just 2 minutes until the peas are cooked (fresh peas will take a couple of minutes longer to cook).

As soon as the vegetables are cooked, transfer to a blender with the chopped mint and cream and whiz until the soup is velvety. Serve.

RACHEL'S TIP
If you are reheating this soup, do so without a lid and don't simmer it for a prolonged time or it will lose its fresh green colour.

IRISH WHISKEY CRÈME BRÛLÉE

A deliciously grown-up end to a meal, it's amazing how just three tablespoons of an Irish whiskey will transform this crème brûlée. Add a hint of grated orange zest to the custard too, if you wish.

Serves 4

FOR THE CUSTARD
300ml (11fl oz) double or regular cream
2 large egg yolks
1 tbsp sugar, plus extra for the top
3 tbsp Irish whiskey

FOR THE CARAMEL
125g (4½oz) caster, granulated or demerara sugar

First make the custard. Pour the cream into a saucepan and heat until almost boiling, then take off the heat.

Place the egg yolks in a heatproof bowl with the sugar and whiskey and whisk thoroughly. Pour the hot cream into the egg yolk mixture, whisking all the time, then tip back into the saucepan on a low–medium heat. Using a wooden spoon or spatula, stir constantly over the heat until it thickens slightly – it should coat the back of the spoon and when you draw a line across the mixture on the spoon, the line will stay without the mixture dripping over.

Pour the custard immediately into your chosen bowls and allow to cool, then place in the fridge; do not cover while it is cooling, and make sure not to break the skin on the top as this is what prevents the caramel from sinking into the custard.

When you're ready to serve the crème brûlées, put 1 teaspoon of sugar on top of each custard, gently spreading it so that it's evenly thick across the whole surface.

Using a blowtorch on full heat, caramelise the sugar in slow circular movements, but take care not to burn it. Allow the caramel to cool and set, then serve. When making the caramel using the blowtorch method the creme brûlées need to be served within 30 minutes.

RACHEL'S TIP
While this is the topping that I prefer on these crème brûlées, as it is lovely and light with just enough crunch, you can, instead, make a caramel in a saucepan, then spoon it over the chilled crèmes. These can be prepared a few hours in advance

since the caramel will be thicker, and also deems the blowtorch unnecessary, so if you don't own one, this is your best option. If using this method, use either caster or granulated sugar. Simply place the sugar (with nothing else) in a medium saucepan on a low–medium heat and stir. As the sugar heats up it will start to look a little strange and grainy, but keep stirring constantly until the sugar turns a rich caramel colour (the colour of whiskey) and becomes viscose. Once the caramel is made, immediately spoon it over the surface of the crèmes in a thin layer, making sure not to swirl it around the top as this can break the surface and the caramel will sink into the crème part.

Allow the caramel to cool and set, then either serve immediately, or store in the fridge or somewhere dry (away from steam) for a few hours.

The name Burren comes from the Irish
word 'Boireann', meaning rocky place,
which seems appropriate as I drive through
the arid stone pavement that makes up
the region and its National Park.

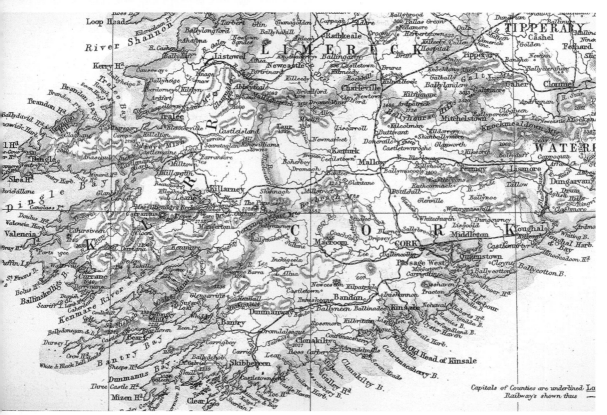

CO. CLARE

AND

THE BURREN

COUNTY CLARE AND THE BURREN

From Dromoland I drive the short journey to the county capital, Ennis. From here, I head towards Kilrush and back towards the Wild Atlantic coast My first stop is Kilkee, just 13km away. I'm at the northern edge of the Loop Head peninsula, lined with soaring cliffs that tumble into the mighty Atlantic below. All of this drama has given me an appetite, and no better place to satisfy it than with some seafood on the terrace at Naughton's Bar. Away to my left from here I can see the white, Caribbean-like sands of Kilkee's enormous beach – which explains its enduring popularity as a seaside resort.

DETOUR: COUNTY CLARE BY FERRY

My favourite way to get to Clare is by ferry. I retrace my journey a little, travelling back towards Limerick and then west, skirting the southern edge of the Shannon estuary as far as Tarbert in northern Kerry. I pass through the village of Askeaton and its set of enchanting ruins – a medieval castle, a friary and a tower built by the Knights Templar – and onwards, past green fields framed by low stone walls. From Tarbert, I and my car board the Shannon Ferry and 20 minutes later I've crossed the mighty Shannon estuary and am at Killimer, right in the heart of south-western Clare.

DETOUR: LOOP HEAD

West of Kilkee, the R487 is signposted as the 'Scenic Loop' and it really doesn't disappoint. On one side are the spectacular cliffs, some with holes blasted in them by a million crashing waves; on the other, the Shannon estuary, a bit of scenic splendour that doesn't get nearly as many visitors as its beauty deserves. Which isn't a bad thing, really: the road gets pretty narrow in parts, wide enough to take only one vehicle. On the south side of the loop is the village of Carrigaholt, overlooked by the ruins of an imposing 15th-century castle. A great stop for a briny bite and traditional music is the Long Dock, which has won awards for its great seafood and is famous for its Carrigaholt oysters, mussels, lobster and chowder. I've no time to sample it on this trip, but when I return home I knock up my own version – Leek, potato, mussel and bacon chowder (see page 195). If you've time, the two-hour dolphin discovery trips run by Dolphinwatch are a great way to see the 100 or so bottlenose dolphins that live in the estuary up close.

I meander slowly up the coast, past the small village of Doonbeg and its golf course and five-star hotel, now carrying Donald Trump's name, and on up to Spanish Point, named after the many sailors who lost their lives when ships from the Spanish Armada ran aground here in 1588 in a terrible storm. There are some lovely walks along the clifftops and down a series of coves and beaches along the coast, where you can breathe in the sea air and feel the spray of the ocean against your face as you walk.

Just a couple of kilometres inland is Miltown Malbay, which comes alive in July during the Willie Clancy Summer School – one of Ireland's most important traditional music festivals. For this, musicians from all over the world come to display their skills in workshops and sessions that last long into the night. In fact, Clare's rich heritage of traditional music is evident all over the county, as I discovered on my travels!

I keep moving northward along the coast, past the surfing paradise of Lahinch and on to Liscannor. Here, with picnic tables set outside for those regular sunny summer days, is the excellent Vaughan's Anchor Inn, which is renowned for its seafood – even the fish 'n' chips is special: the perfectly battered cod comes with chips that have been steamed then fried in beef dripping and served with a homemade tartare sauce and a pea puree … delicious! The aroma of frying fish fills my nose, and my mouth begins to water. This is what I remember when I fashion my own fish and chips at home, dipping fish fresh from the sea into a beer-laced batter that gives a crisp, light coating (see page 202).

After lunch, I tackle one of Ireland's big-ticket attractions – the Cliffs of Moher, 203m of vertiginous natural splendour that are forever lapped by a churning sea at their base. They're incredibly popular, and tourists clamour to get a good view from the top. I get away from the worst of these crowds by following the trail south past the Moher Wall as far as Hag's Head – it's a good thing I have a head for heights as the walk is not for the fainthearted!

You can visit the cliffs from the sea on a boat from Doolin, just 6km up the coast, but I'm staying on dry land and checking out some of the town's famous music pubs – McGann's, O'Connor's and MacDiarmada's – which get very crowded when the traditional music is in full swing!

North of here, the landscape changes dramatically. I'm entering The Burren, a limestone landscape stripped of green but no less beautiful for it, especially in spring when the wildflowers are in bloom and the whole region is speckled in colour. The name Burren comes from the Irish word 'Boireann', meaning rocky place, which seems appropriate as I drive through the arid stone pavement that makes up the region and its National Park.

En route, just outside Lisdoonvarna, the town made famous by the yearly matchmaking festival, I stop at the Burren Smokehouse and meet with Birgitta and Peter Curtin, who began oak-smoking salmon here in 1989. I linger over lunch, tempted by the mixed plate of salmon, mackerel and trout. I long to pick up a fully stocked hamper and go for a picnic, but instead I settle for ordering some smoked salmon. When I finish the road trip, this becomes an essential ingredient for Smoked salmon and kale soufflé omelette (see page 197) – every bite reminds me of this stop in Lisdoonvarna.

The Burren might seem empty and arid now, but in ancient times it was full of people – there are over 2,500 prehistoric monuments scattered throughout the region. I make my way to the most famous monument of all, the Poulnabrone Dolmen – also known as the Portal Tomb – a 5,000-year-old grave topped by a 5-tonne capstone. I stand and admire it, gazing upwards at the huge stone that tops off the columns. Grey and imposing, it's mightily impressive, and all I can think about as I stand there is how did they manage to lift such a heavy rock without a crane?

My next stop is at the Burren Perfumery and Floral Centre in Carron, 6km from Poulnabrone. All of the gorgeous scents created here are inspired by the plants and aromas of the Burren, and I'm surprised to discover that the area is full of orchids growing among the rocks!

My final stop for the day is Ballyvaughan, 17km to the north of Carron and back on the coast. My destination is Gregan's Castle Hotel, 6km south of town at Corkscrew Hill. This wonderful 19th-century manor home has 20 fabulous rooms and a well-respected restaurant that serves delicious, locally sourced cuisine. I settle in for the night and discover that many an illustrious predecessor has stayed here, including J.R.R. Tolkien, who must have drawn inspiration from the Burren for *The Lord of the Rings* – I wonder if he ever visited one of the area's myriad caves, called Pol na Gollum?

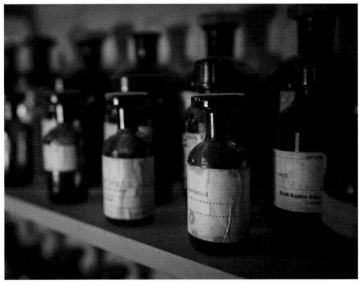

LEEK, POTATO, MUSSEL AND BACON CHOWDER

A simple, lovely bowl of comforting goodness. All it needs is some crusty bread on the side.

Serves 4–6 as a starter

30g (1¼oz) butter
100g (3½oz) streaky bacon rashers (smoked or unsmoked), all rind and bones removed, meat cut into 1cm (½in) pieces
100g (3½oz) leeks, trimmed, washed and finely chopped
500g (1lb 2oz) peeled potatoes, chopped into 1cm (½in) dice
500ml (18fl oz) hot chicken stock
750g (1lb 10oz) mussels in their shells, well washed and cleaned – discard any that are not tightly shut or don't close when tapped
100ml (3½fl oz) double or regular cream
2 tbsp chopped chives
a little squeeze of lemon juice
1 tbsp chopped parsley leaves

Melt the butter in a saucepan on a medium heat. Add the bacon and fry for about 5 minutes, until golden. Add the leeks and potatoes, cover and cook for about 10 minutes until the potatoes are almost tender. Add the hot stock and continue to cook until the potatoes are cooked.

Tip in the mussels, cover and cook for about 5 minutes until their shells open, shaking the pan occasionally. Discard any mussels that remain closed.

Stir in the cream and chives and a few drops of lemon juice, then heat through. Sprinkle the parsley over the top and serve in warm bowls.

SMOKED SALMON AND KALE SOUFFLÉ OMELETTE

This is a dream of an omelette. Light and fluffy, rich and luxurious – perfect for a special brunch or supper.

Serves 2–3 as brunch, lunch or supper

30g (1¼oz) butter
125g (4½oz) smoked salmon, cut into 1–2cm (½–¾in) pieces
40g (1½oz) kale (weighed after the stalks are removed)
salt and freshly ground black pepper
5 eggs
pinch of freshly grated nutmeg
50ml (2fl oz) double or regular cream
25g (1oz) finely grated hard cheese, such as extra-mature Coolea, Corleggy or
    Parmesan

Place a 25.5cm (10in) diameter frying pan on a medium–high heat. Add half the butter and allow to melt, then add the smoked salmon and, as it cooks, bash it up a bit with a wooden spoon into slightly chunky flakes. The salmon will be cooked in about 3 minutes and should be opaque all the way through. Spoon the salmon out of the pan into a bowl, leaving the butter in the pan.

Shred the kale leaves and place in a pan with a pinch of salt and enough boiling water to cover. Cook, uncovered, on a high heat for 2 minutes until just tender, then drain and squeeze out the excess water. Chop coarsely and add to the salmon.

Separate the eggs and add the egg yolks to the salmon and kale. Stir in the nutmeg and some salt and pepper to season, then mix in 1 tablespoon of the cream and half the grated cheese. Whisk the egg whites in a clean, grease-free bowl until stiff.

Place the frying pan back on a medium heat, add the remaining butter and allow to melt. Fold the egg whites into the salmon mixture and gently tip into the pan. Cook for a few minutes until the omelette is golden underneath.

Preheat the grill.

Pour the remaining cream all over the top of the omelette and scatter with the cheese. Place under the grill and cook for a few minutes until golden on top and very slightly set. It should feel like a very light and soft marshmallow in the centre when you gently press it with your finger.

Slide the omelette out of the pan onto your serving plate and cut into slices to serve. Serve on its own or with a green salad.

STOUT-BRAISED BEEF CHEEKS WITH CAVOLO NERO

Just the name of this recipe sounds generous and hearty, and that's exactly what it is. A big, comforting, wintery stew that would just love to be washed down with a glass of your favourite Irish stout.

Serves 4–6 as a main course

2 beef cheeks, about 750g (1lb 10oz) total weight (each beef cheek weighs about
    375g/13oz), cut into 3cm (1¼in) chunks
125g (4½oz) smoked bacon, cut into 2cm (¾in) pieces
salt and freshly ground black pepper
2 tbsp olive oil
200g (7oz) leeks, trimmed, washed, halved lengthways and cut into
    1cm (½in) slices
200g (7oz) celery, trimmed and cut into 1cm (½in) slices
6 cloves of garlic, peeled and sliced
200ml (7fl oz) Irish stout
200ml (7fl oz) chicken or beef stock
200g (7oz) cavolo nero (weight with stalks)

Preheat the oven to 170°C (325°F), Gas mark 3.

Place a flameproof casserole or ovenproof saucepan with a lid on a medium–high heat. Season the beef cheeks and bacon with salt and pepper and put into the hot pan with the olive oil. Brown the meat on both sides, then remove from the pan. Add the leeks, celery and garlic to the pan and season, then cook for 3–4 minutes until light golden. Return the beef cheeks and bacon to the pan and add the stout and stock and bring to the boil. Cover the pan, transfer to the oven and cook for 3 hours until the beef is meltingly tender. Once the beef is cooked, use a slotted spoon to transfer the beef and bacon to a plate.

Tip all the juices and vegetables into a sieve placed over a bowl and push through to get a smooth sauce. Pour the sauce back into the casserole, add the beef and bacon and bring to the boil on the hob.

Remove and discard the cavolo nero stalks, then shred the leaves. Add the leaves to the casserole, stir, cover and cook for 1–2 minutes until the kale is tender.

Serve with creamy mashed potatoes.

CRISPY BEER BATTER

While the flavour of the beer isn't very obvious in the batter (as the alcohol evaporates in the heat of the oil), the lovely big bubbles give a coating to fried fish that is wonderfully crisp and light.

Makes enough to coat 4 medium fish fillets

100g (3½oz) self-raising flour
good pinch of salt
150ml (5fl oz) beer, lager or ale (not stout)

Sift the flour and salt into a bowl, then whisk in the beer, making sure you don't have any lumps.

Dunk in a piece of spanking fresh fish and deep fry. Serve with a flavoured or plain mayonnaise.

We now have quite a few really great artisan salt producers in Ireland, who boil, each in their own specialised way, the fresh seawater down to practically nothing to give us our most commonly used seasoning. While it's not the fastest thing to produce, I urge you all to make your own salt at least once – I promise you'll treasure it!

Makes 20g (¾oz) salt

1 litre (1¾ pints) seawater

Pour the seawater into a saucepan just big enough to take it. Place on a hob on a high heat and bring to the boil. Turn the heat down slightly and continue to boil, uncovered, until it reduces to an almost dry salty mix. As it reduces, stir, or rather scrape the bottom of the pan with a wooden spatula to release the salt. It will take anything from 45 minutes–2 hours, depending on the size of the pan and the heat of the flame.

When the mixture looks thick and sandy, turn the heat down to very low and cook until it dries a little, then take off the heat and allow it to sit in the pan. As it sits it will continue to dry out more – until you have dry salt! Store in a clean dry jar.

Apples
8 for £3-
15 for £5-

TOFFEE APPLE PUDDING

A great family-style pudding. I love this technique where a sugar-water mixture is poured over the raw sweet batter before it goes in the oven, to produce a delicious pudding sitting on a rich toffee sauce.

Serves 4

100g (3½oz) plain flour
2 tsp baking powder
50g (2oz) caster sugar
pinch of salt
100ml (3½fl oz) milk
50g (2oz) unsalted butter, melted
1 egg
1 tsp vanilla extract
1 large cooking apple, such as Bramley, peeled, quartered, cored and chopped
    into 2cm (¾in) dice
75g (3oz) brown sugar
125ml (4½fl oz) boiling water

Preheat the oven to 180°C (350°F), Gas mark 4.

Sift the flour and baking powder into a bowl, then mix in the caster sugar and salt. Make a well in the centre.

In another bowl, whisk together the milk, melted butter, egg and vanilla extract.

Place the apple chunks in a 1 litre (1¾ pint) gratin dish and spread out to cover the base.

Pour the wet ingredients into the dry ingredients and whisk to mix completely. Pour this over the apples, evenly, to cover.

Next, mix the brown sugar with the boiling water and drizzle all over the batter. This will sink in during baking and form a delicious toffee sauce. Bake for 25 minutes or until the sponge is set.

Serve with vanilla ice cream or softly whipped cream.

BUTTERMILK CARDAMOM CAKE

I love the subtle acidic tang that buttermilk brings to baking, and because that acidity tenderises the gluten in the flour, you get a cake with a lovely soft texture that just works beautifully with the aromatic cardamom in this recipe.

Serves 6–8

FOR THE CAKE

125g (4½oz) unsalted butter, softened, plus extra for greasing

225g (8oz) caster sugar

3 eggs

200ml (7fl oz) buttermilk

finely grated zest of 1 lemon

1 tsp ground cardamom seeds (from 10 green cardamom pods)

¾ tsp salt

250g (9oz) plain flour

½ tsp baking powder

¼ tsp bicarbonate of soda

FOR THE ICING

260–280g (9½–generous 10oz) icing sugar

2 tbsp buttermilk

½ tsp ground cardamom seeds (from 5 green cardamom pods)

1 tbsp lemon juice

Preheat the oven to 180°C (350°F), Gas mark 4. Line the base of a 23cm (9in) spring-form cake tin with a disc of baking parchment or greaseproof paper and grease the sides with butter.

Put the butter and caster sugar in a bowl and beat until soft. Beat in the eggs one at a time, then mix in the buttermilk, lemon zest, cardamom and salt. Sift in the flour, baking powder and bicarbonate of soda and mix. Spoon into the prepared tin and bake for 40 minutes or until golden on top and a skewer inserted into the centre of the cake comes out clean. Take out of the oven and allow to sit in the tin for 10 minutes.

To remove the cake from the tin, run a small sharp knife around the side of the cake, carefully unclip the sides and remove. Take a plate, but not your serving plate, tip the cake over onto it, and remove the base of the tin and the sheet of parchment. Then take your cake serving plate, put it over the cake and flip it over.

Next, make the icing. Place the icing sugar in a bowl, add the buttermilk, cardamom and lemon juice and mix well. You may need a further 25g (1oz) of icing sugar.

When the cake is cool and on your chosen cake plate, using a palette knife or back of a spoon (dipped in boiling water to help it if you need it), spread the icing over the top of the cake. It may drizzle a little over the edges. Allow the icing to set for about 10 minutes, then serve.

Native oysters have been farmed here since prehistoric times, and in each of them you can taste the unique flavours that make them special: the hint of Burren limestone, Connemara sandstone and the Atlantic brine.

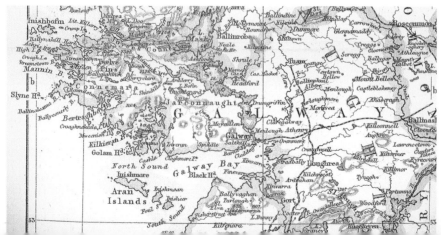

GALWAY CITY AND LOUGH CORRIB

GALWAY CITY AND LOUGH CORRIB

I bid farewell to The Burren and make my way to Galway City. Before I reach the City of the Tribes, though, I have to make an important stop, if only to see at source one of the briny delicacies Galway is famous for ...

The 2.5km stretch between Kilcolgan and Clarinbridge is the heartland of Galway's oyster farming. Here, from late November to the end of December, 60 boats manned by local farmers take part in dredging season, throwing back any oysters less than three inches in diameter. The dredged oysters are then bought by about five local dealers, who age them in their own steeping grounds before selling them on to restaurants, both local and beyond.

Native oysters have been farmed here since prehistoric times, and in each of them you can taste the unique flavours that make them special: the hint of Burren limestone, Connemara sandstone and the Atlantic brine. Today these oysters are a much sought-after delicacy; it's a far cry from a century ago and more, when they were considered the poor man's food and sustained many a family during the Famine.

The Kelly family in Kilcolgan has been farming oysters for over 60 years. Michael Kelly started with Native oysters; his sons Michael and Diarmuid have broadened the business to include Gigas (or Pacific) oysters, mussels and clams. I pay a quick visit to see how they farm but then I make my way down the road to Moran's On the Weir, where I enjoy a fine half dozen of Native oysters in the half-shell and I'm in heaven.

Satisfied, I get back on the road and head up to Galway City itself. It's a city designed for wandering, meandering through the streets, soaking up the sounds of the city. Small enough for foot power, there are alleys and little side streets that are perfect to get (momentarily) lost in; no matter where you are, you're never far from everywhere else.

The obvious place to wander is along the pedestrianised streets west of Eyre Square – Shop Street, Mainguard Street and High Street. Two of the city's best-known pubs are here, Tig Cóili and the always full Séhán Ua Neáchtain, but if I'm looking for a slightly less frenetic spot to enjoy some traditional music I make my way across the Corrib to the Crane Bar; the upstairs lounge has the music, while downstairs a meditative silence prevails.

It's once again time for food – and Galway is a slice of gourmet heaven. Galway's specialty, inevitably, is not just oysters, but seafood in general. You'll find it on virtually every menu, whether it's perfectly cooked salmon or a late-night fish and chips after an evening in one of the pubs. The city's bustling market runs every Saturday (Sundays, too, in summer, and every day during the

Galway Festival) and it's a great spot to find locally made goodies that would be ideal in a picnic hamper, from crêpes to sushi.

Right by Spanish Arch, Ard Bia At Nimmo's is a long-time favourite: inside the stone-built medieval customs house, Aoibheann MacNamara has maintained a strict commitment to the very best of local produce, and the proof is in the proverbial pudding. The dishes are prepared using the best of local ingredients, influenced by recipes from across the world. Wild garlic is served with polenta, local spring lamb is finished with a Mediterranean-style gremolata and tzatziki, and mascarpone combines with local honey for a creamy dessert. The menu is ever changing, but always good. The Mediterranean flavours inspire my Irish version of a great Italian dessert – Carrageen panna cotta (see page 231).

I also like Kai Café + Restaurant where I'm a huge fan of Jess Murphy's cooking – all made from local produce, of course, and a restaurant at the forefront of Ireland's organic food movement. Another firm favourite is J.P. MacManus's cooking at Aniar, which also makes extraordinary use of local produce, but I'm not alone in thinking this: J.P. and his wife Drigín's beautifully relaxed restaurant earned itself a Michelin star, Galway's first! Enda McEvoy has recently opened his restaurant Loam, which is also well worth a visit. I'll also make sure to pop into Sheridan's, who sell the best selection of cheese in the best condition here at their flagship shop and their others around Ireland too. I find some gorgeous mature Coolea (from West Cork) and a great bottle of red wine, trying to avoid the jewel-coloured chutneys and delicious chocolates that also beg for my attention! The Coolea is an ingredient I sneak into lots of dishes, here as a finishing touch to Fresh pasta ribbons with wild garlic, olive oil and butter (see page 226). It is Ireland's answer to Parmesan and for me it inspires many an Irish-Italian dish.

Galway is famous for its festivals, celebrating the arts, film, music and, of course, food. In September the city goes mad for the Calrenbridge Oyster Festivaland the Galway Oyster Festival: three days of shucking, slurping and salivating that climaxes in the World Oyster Opening Championships – the current record-holder has 233 shucks in three minutes!

A LOBSTER SUPPER

One of the best meals I've ever eaten that seems to pop into my mind time and time again was a picnic on the beach near where we live. Everything seems to taste great when eaten out in the elements, and when the food is also cooked outside, it is even better.

We cooked lobster in seawater in a pot over an open fire. After removing the meat from the shell, we devoured the lobster with some delicious mayonnaise we had brought, as well as some tomatoes with basil, cucumber pickle and boiled new potatoes. So simple, but totally unforgettable. This has to be my favourite summertime meal ever.

Serves 2–4

2 medium live lobsters, placed in the freezer for two hours
salt

FOR THE COURT BOUILLON
1 carrot, sliced
1 onion, peeled and sliced
1 stick of celery, trimmed and sliced
600ml (1 pint) dry white wine
few parsley stalks
few sprigs of thyme
1 bay leaf

Put the lobsters in a large pan, cover with measured lukewarm water and add about 2 tablespoons of salt to every 1.75 litres (3 pints) water. Put on a medium heat and bring the water slowly to a simmer, 10–20 minutes; at this stage the lobsters will be dead and just starting to change colour. Drain all the water from the pan.

Place all the court bouillon ingredients in the saucepan with the lobsters and add 600ml (1 pint) water. Cover the pan and bring to the boil, then cook for 20–30 minutes until the lobsters have turned bright orange. Remove them from the pot and allow to cool slightly before removing the meat. (I sometimes strain the cooking liquid and add a tiny bit to the mayonnaise.)

To remove the meat from the shells, place a boiled lobster, belly side up, on a chopping board. While holding the lobster firmly with one hand, place the tip of a large sharp chopping knife into the centre of its head, with the tip of the knife facing away from the tail. Using quite a bit of pressure, press down firmly to slice the lobster in half, lengthways.

Though the head contains all the delicious and sweet brown meat, there is a small gritty stomach sack behind the mouth that you should discard.

All down the tail is the wonderful white meat, which is just like an oversized prawn, and in the head the brown meat consists of the greyish greeny-brown (tasting a lot better than it sounds!) soft-textured meat. This can be eaten on its own or is great mixed with a little mayonnaise and served with the tail. The meat from the claws (which need to be cracked with the back of a sharp knife, a nut cracker or lobster claw crackers) is also divine and different in texture to that of the tail.

The split lobster looks great just as it is, still attached to its shell, sitting on plates; I love to serve it just like this and let people pick out the meat themselves, making sure there are some skewers and nutrackers on the table, and not forgetting finger bowls and a larger bowl for discarded shells.

TOMATO AND BASIL SALAD

Serves 2–4

5 vine-ripened tomatoes, each sliced into 5mm
  (¼in) rounds
4 tbsp best extra virgin olive oil
good squeeze of lemon juice
salt and freshly ground black pepper
pinch of caster sugar
2 tbsp torn or sliced basil

Arrange the tomatoes on a serving dish. Dress with the olive oil and lemon juice and season with salt, pepper and sugar. Just before serving, sprinkle the tomatoes with the basil.

CUCUMBER PICKLE

Serves 2–4

450g (1lb) thinly sliced unpeeled cucumber
1 small onion, peeled and thinly sliced
175g (6oz) caster sugar
1 tbsp salt
125ml (4½fl oz) cider vinegar or white wine vinegar

Mix the cucumber and onion in a large bowl, add the sugar, salt and vinegar and mix well to combine. Taste and, if necessary, adjust the sharpness by adding more vinegar or sugar. Make 1 hour ahead, if possible. This will keep in the fridge for up to a month.

MAYONNAISE

Makes 300ml (11fl oz)

2 egg yolks
pinch of salt
1 tsp Dijon mustard
2 tsp white wine vinegar
200ml (7fl oz) sunflower oil
25ml (1fl oz) extra virgin olive oil
freshly ground black pepper
2 tbsp chopped herbs, such as chives, dill, fennel
  (optional)

Place the egg yolks in a bowl, then mix in the salt, mustard and vinegar.

Mix the oils together in a jug and very gradually, whisking all the time (either by hand or using a hand-held electric beater), slowly add to the egg yolks. You should start to see the mixture thickening. Season with pepper and more salt to taste, then stir in the chopped herbs, if you wish.

BOILED NEW POTATOES

Serves 2–4

500g (1lb 2oz) new potatoes, skins scrubbed but not
  peeled
½ tsp salt
sprig of fresh mint
15g (½oz) butter

Place a pan of water on a high heat and bring to the boil, then add the potatoes, salt and mint. Boil for 15–30 minutes depending on the size of the potatoes, until tender to the point of a knife.

Drain and serve with the butter divided between servings.

PAN-FRIED RAY WITH HAZELNUT GREMOLATA

The ray, like skate, is closely related to the shark and because of its rich, almost gelatinous texture it works superbly with this nutty, citrusy sauce.

Serves 2 as a main course

1 ray wing, about 400g (14oz), on the bone, skin on
salt
100g (3½oz) soft butter

FOR THE HAZELNUT GREMOLATA
15g (½oz) hazelnuts, roasted, peeled and chopped (see page 295)
1 tsp cider vinegar
finely grated zest of ½ lemon
2 tbsp chopped parsley leaves
pinch of salt
twist of black pepper

Choose a pan large and wide enough to fit the whole ray wing. Add the wing and fill with enough measured water to cover the ray, then add 1 teaspoon of salt to each 1.2 litres (2 pints) water.

Bring the water to the boil, then turn the heat down and simmer the ray wing for 10 minutes or until the skin can just come away from the flesh. Using a large fish slice, carefully lift the fish out onto a tray. Allow to cool slightly, then peel off the skin from both sides. Leave to cool a little. Drain the pan.

Meanwhile, put the hazelnuts in a small pan on a medium heat until warm, then add the vinegar and allow to evaporate. Put the hazelnuts in a bowl with all the remaining gremolata ingredients.

Rub the fillets on both sides with a little of the soft butter, then return them to their pan and fry, turning once, until golden on each side. Transfer to two warm plates. Add the hazelnut gremolata to the pan with the remaining butter. Allow it to foam and bubble, then add 1 tablespoon of water to loosen. Pour the contents of the pan over the fish and serve.

RACHEL'S TIP
This sauce is also great with scallops in place of the ray.

RAY FINGERS WITH MINT, TARRAGON AND CAPER MAYONNAISE

Ray and chips has been a favourite in Irish chippers for decades and for good reason, too. In this recipe the fish is first filleted, then, to give a delicious crunchy coating, tossed in flour, egg and breadcrumbs before being fried.

Serves 4 as a starter, or 2 as a main course

1 ray wing, about 400g (14oz), on the bone, skin on

salt

100g (3½oz) seasoned plain flour

2–3 eggs, beaten

100g (3½oz) fresh breadcrumbs

2 tbsp extra virgin olive oil

2 tbsp butter

FOR THE MINT, TARRAGON AND CAPER MAYONNAISE

1 tbsp chopped mint

1 tbsp chopped tarragon

2 cloves of garlic, peeled and crushed

good pinch of salt

good twist of black pepper

2 egg yolks

2 tsp Dijon mustard

1 tsp lemon juice

175ml (6fl oz) sunflower oil

75ml (3fl oz) extra virgin olive oil

1 tbsp capers, chopped

1 spring onion, chopped, or 2 tsp chives, snipped

Choose a pan large and wide enough to fit the whole wing, then add the wing and fill the pan with enough measured water to cover the ray. Add 1 teaspoon of salt to each 1.2 litres (2 pints) water.

Bring the water to the boil, then turn the heat down and simmer the wing for 10 minutes or until the skin can just come away from the flesh. Using a large fish slice, carefully lift the fish out onto a tray. Allow to cool slightly, then peel off the skin from both sides and leave to cool a little.

Meanwhile, make the mayonnaise. Put the herbs, garlic, salt and pepper in a pestle and mortar and pound to a fine paste. Put the paste in a small bowl and mix in the egg yolks, mustard and lemon juice. Mix the oils together in a jug and very gradually, whisking all the time (either by hand or using a hand-held electric beater), slowly add to the egg yolks to make a mayonnaise. Stir in the chopped capers and chives or spring onions and taste to check the seasoning.

Place a frying pan on a high heat and allow to get hot. Lift the fillet from the bone on each side of the ray and divide each into 4 equal pieces (they will look like long fingers), 2–3cm (½–1¼in) wide. Put the seasoned flour, beaten eggs and breadcrumbs in individual bowls big enough to toss the fish in. Carefully coat each piece with the flour, then the beaten egg and, finally, the breadcrumbs.

Combine the olive oil and butter in the hot pan and pan-fry each piece of fish on both sides until golden. Transfer to warm plates and serve with the mint, tarragon and caper mayonnaise. If serving as a main course it would be good with some little fries or a green salad.

SPAGHETTI WITH CLAMS, GIN AND WILD GARLIC

A super-fast, super-delicious pasta dish that gets its inspiration from the Italian spaghetti alle vongole. Use lots of chives in place of the wild garlic when not in season.

Serves 4 as a main course

1 generous tsp salt
325g (11½oz) dried spaghetti or 400g (14oz) fresh spaghetti
1kg (2lb 2oz) clams in their shells, well washed and scrubbed –
    discard any that are not tightly shut or don't close when tapped
60ml (2½fl oz) gin
3 cloves of garlic, peeled and sliced very thinly
160ml (5½fl oz) double or regular cream
4 tbsp chopped wild garlic, plus 2 tbsp to serve
juice of ½ lemon

Place a medium–large saucepan of water on to boil and add the salt. When it comes up to the boil, add the spaghetti, stir and cook for 8 minutes (for dried pasta) or until al dente. Fresh pasta will cook much faster.

Strain the pasta, leaving 50ml (2fl oz) of the cooking water in the saucepan to prevent the pasta from getting sticky, then return the spaghetti to the pan. Set aside while you cook the clams (or you can cook the clams while the spaghetti is cooking).

Place the clams, gin and sliced garlic in a large wide saucepan on a medium–high heat, cover with a lid and cook for 3–4 minutes until the clams have opened. Discard any clams that remain closed. Using tongs or a slotted spoon, pick out the clams and drop them into the spaghetti.

Add the cream to the sliced garlic and gin and boil for 1–2 minutes until slightly thickened (not too thick or you'll need to add a splash of water), then add the wild garlic and lemon juice.

Tip the spaghetti and clams into the sauce, stir over the heat for a few seconds, then serve with extra wild garlic sprinkled over the top.

DUCK BREAST WITH WHITE BEAN RAGOUT

The rich dark meat of the duck breast sits very happily beside this delicious accompaniment of beans, bacon and fennel. A wonderfully hearty but truly elegant main course. Serve on its own or with roast or mashed potatoes.

Serves 6 as a main course

240g (8½oz) dried beans (cannellini, pinto or haricot), soaked in cold water, to
    cover, overnight, or 2 x 400g tins, drained and rinsed
1 tbsp extra virgin olive oil
150g (5oz) back bacon, chopped into small lardons, 0.5 x 2cm (¼ x ¾in)
25g (1oz) butter
1 clove of garlic, peeled and chopped
250g (9oz) fennel bulb, trimmed and finely diced
250g (9oz) carrots, peeled and finely diced
250g (9oz) red onion, peeled and finely diced
1 tbsp chopped sage
175ml (6fl oz) white wine
400ml (14fl oz) chicken or duck stock
125ml (4½fl oz) double or regular cream
4–6 duck breasts, depending on size, criss-cross scored in the fat, but not flesh
salt and freshly ground black pepper

Drain the soaked beans and place in a saucepan. Cover with cold water, bring to a boil on a high heat, then cook for 45–60 minutes until tender. Drain.

Heat the olive oil and gently fry the lardons until just crisping at the edges, then add the butter, garlic, fennel, carrots and red onion. Cover and cook gently, on a low heat, until soft. Turn the heat to high, uncover the pan and add the beans, sage, wine and stock. Bring to the boil and reduce by half, then add the cream, allow to bubble and set aside.

Season the duck, then place, skin side down, in a cold pan on a low–medium heat. As the pan heats up, drain off the rendered fat (save it in a jar), until the skin is golden brown, 15–20 minutes. Don't let the pan get too hot or the skin will burn before the fat renders out. Turn the heat to high, turn over the duck and fry until brown, a few minutes. Transfer to a warm plate to rest for 10–15 minutes.

Reheat the beans and vegetables, slice the duck breasts thinly and divide among the plates with a couple of spoonfuls of the beans and vegetables.

FRESH PASTA RIBBONS, WILD GARLIC, OLIVE OIL AND BUTTER

Fresh handmade pasta doesn't need much. In fact, the less adornment the better, and it's hard to think of a more delicious way of enjoying the wild garlic that we get in springtime.

Serves 4 as a main course

1 x quantity homemade pasta (see overleaf), or 300g (11oz) dried pasta
salt and freshly ground black pepper
3 tbsp extra virgin olive oil, plus extra for drizzling over at the end
25g (1oz) butter
4 cloves of garlic, peeled and finely sliced
300g (11oz) wild garlic leaves, cut lengthways into 2 or 3 slices
pinch of freshly grated nutmeg
50g (2oz) finely grated hard cheese, such as mature Coolea or Parmesan

First, make the pasta following the recipe overleaf. Roll out the dough to 1.5–2cm (5/8–¾in) wide and, using a serrated pastry wheel or a sharp-bladed knife, cut into ribbons. Place a large saucepan of salted water on a high heat to boil.

Meanwhile, place a wide frying pan on a high heat and add the 3 tablespoons of olive oil and the butter. When melted and hot, add the sliced garlic and stir for just a few seconds until the garlic turns very light golden, then immediately add the wild garlic leaves, nutmeg and salt and pepper to season. Stir for a few seconds until the leaves wilt, then take off the heat and set aside.

Place the pasta in the boiling salted water and stir, then bring back to the boil, uncovered. If you're using fresh pasta it will take just a couple of minutes to cook; if it's dried it will take longer.

Once the pasta is al dente, strain it but reserve about 200ml (7fl oz) of the cooking water (you may not need all of it). Pour 25ml (1fl oz) of the cooking water into the pasta, stir and set aside briefly.

Place the pan of wild garlic back on a high heat and allow to get hot, then add the pasta to it (if the wild garlic pan is not large enough to take all the pasta you'll need to do it the other way round). Add 50–75ml (2–3fl oz) of the pasta cooking water to the pan – just enough to get it a little bit juicy and steamy. Taste for seasoning, adding more salt, pepper or nutmeg if necessary.

Tip into a wide warm serving bowl, drizzle with a little more olive oil, scatter with the grated cheese and serve.

HOMEMADE PASTA

Makes about 600g (1lb 6oz) pasta, serves 5-6
(keep any uncooked leftover pasta in an airtight box in the fridge for another day)

400g (14oz) '00' flour
100g (3½oz) semolina flour, plus extra for rolling out and dusting
2 tsp salt
3 whole eggs and 2 egg yolks

Place the '00' flour, the semolina flour and salt into a bowl, mix, and make a well in the centre. Drop the eggs and egg yolks into the centre and mix in the flour and semolina, using your fingertips to rub it together. When the mixture is at a crumbly stage (before you form it into a ball of dough), check to see if there is enough moisture in it by squeezing a little piece together. It should be quite dry and just about able to come together. If it doesn't stick together, add a little egg white, but be careful as the dough should be really quite dry. Bring it together to form a ball of dough (this should be quite difficult as it's not a wet dough) and knead for 8–10 minutes or until really smooth. Wrap the ball of dough in cling film or pop it into a plastic bag and set aside to rest for 30 minutes before rolling.

Cut the dough into four pieces, keeping the rest covered while you roll out each ball. I use a pasta rolling machine, and this is definitely the most convenient way to do it, but it is possible to use a rolling pin and roll the dough in a few pieces on your worktop. While rolling the dough, either with a rolling pin, or using a pasta machine, lightly dust the dough every so often with a little semolina flour. You won't need much as the dough shouldn't be sticky. Roll the dough until it is 1–2mm thick.

Using a serrated pastry wheel, cut the rolled-out dough into 1.5cm wide (5/8 in) strips. If you don't have a pastry wheel, just use a sharp-bladed knife.

I like to hang the pasta for about an hour to let it dry out a little as it will keep better if it's slightly dry. I normally place the pasta, in a single layer, over the handle of a (clean!) broom balanced between two stools or chairs.

You can cook the pasta immediately, or toss them in a little semolina flour then place on a tray or an airtight box to store for up to 3 days.

CARRAGEEN PANNA COTTA

This takes its influence from the classic Italian panna cotta (which means cooked cream), but is set, instead of with gelatine, with the Irish seaweed carrageen (which, incidentally, means 'little rock', because when the tide goes out that's exactly where it can be found).

Serves 4–6

8g (1/3oz) carrageen (this fills my semi-closed fist)
400ml (14fl oz) double or regular cream
200ml (7fl oz) milk
50g (2oz) caster or granulated sugar, plus extra for sprinkling
1 tsp vanilla extract or 1 vanilla pod, slightly split
fresh raspberries, and hulled and quartered straberries, to serve

Put a small plate in your freezer.

Place the carrageen in a bowl, cover with tepid water and soak for 10 minutes. Drain, then put the carrageen in a saucepan with the cream, milk, sugar and vanilla pod (if using). Don't add the extract yet. Stir on a medium heat and bring to the boil, then cover, turn the heat down and simmer for 5 minutes. Take off the heat.

Take the plate out of the freezer and place a small spoonful of the carrageen mixture on it, then pop it back in the freezer for 1 minute. Take out and run your finger through it – it should be set. If it is still runny, place the mixture back on the heat and cook for a further minute before testing again.

Pour the mixture through a sieve (you can wash the vanilla pod and use it again another time) but don't push the seaweed through the sieve, just the liquid that is clinging to it. Scrape the mixture from under the sieve and, using a whisk, mix it with the drained cream mixture and the vanilla extract (if using). Pour into four or six small bowls or glasses and place in the fridge to set.

Serve with some raspberries or sliced strawberries (which have been scattered with sugar) on top.

On a clear day, the views of Clifden Bay and its two offshore islands, Inishturk and Turbot, are spectacular. I pull over and enjoy my crab sandwich in the ideal setting.

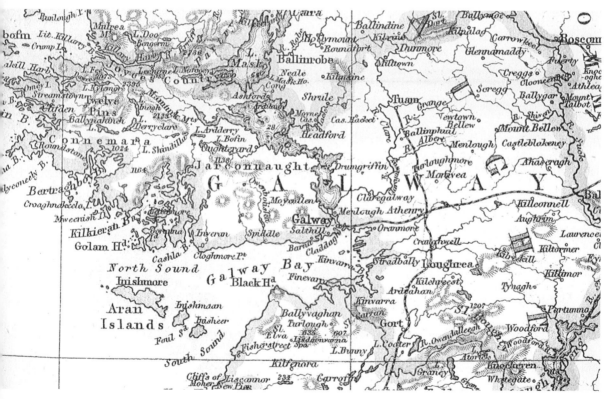

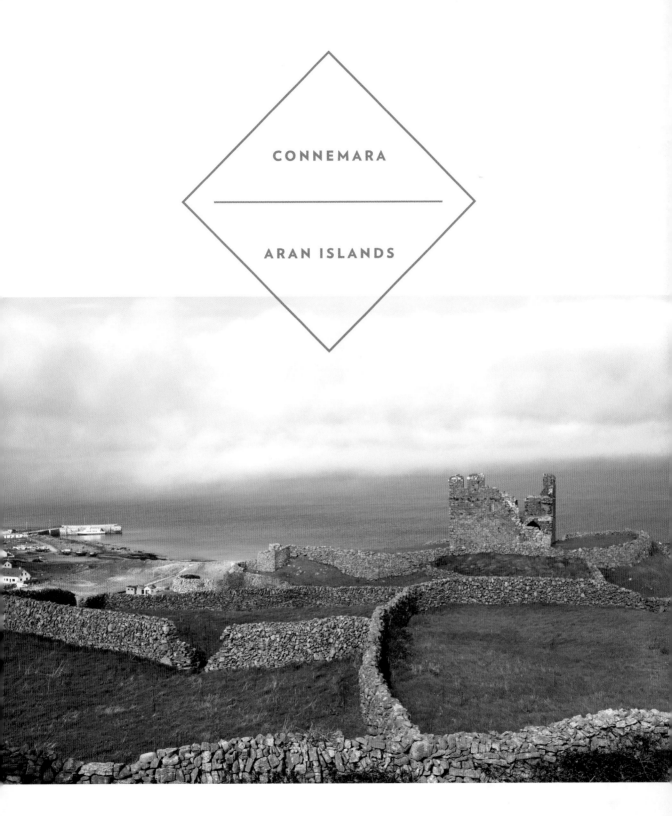

CONNEMARA

ARAN ISLANDS

CONNEMARA AND THE ARAN ISLANDS

Leave Galway I must, so I make my way down the western side of the lough and head west into Connemara proper. I drive through Salthill, out along the coastal road past Barna and Furbogh, through Irish-speaking An Spidéal, perhaps stopping for tea and cake at Builin Blasta – 'the tasty loaf' – in the Ceardlann Design Centre.

West of town is the gateway to Connemara: the fields are criss-crossed by low stone walls and the scenery stretches out to reveal itself in all its dramatic beauty. A few kilometres further on is the airstrip at Minna, near Inverin, where I'm going to make the first of my Connemara detours with a 10-minute flight across Galway Bay to the Aran Islands.

Each of the islands is worth exploring – Inishmór has the prehistoric fort of Dún Aengus and the bulk of the visitors; Inisheer, the smallest of the islands, is a walker's paradise, especially if you do the 12km coastal route. But today I'm opting for Inishmaan, the least-visited of the islands.

Early Christian monks came here looking for contemplative solitude, as did author J.M. Synge centuries later: the monks left a stone church as evidence of their being here, while Synge bequeathed us two of his best-known plays – *Riders to the Sea* and *The Playboy of the Western World* – which were both inspired by his stay here. And you can see why: its tranquility soothes you from the moment you step onto the island, and the sounds of civilisation are but a distant hum. At the island's western edge is Synge's Chair, a sheltered lookout at the edge of a sheer limestone cliff – the perfect spot to take in the wildness of the islands without interruption.

I opt for something a little more contemporary and make my way to Inis Meáin, Ruairí de Blacam and his wife Marie-Thérèse's stunning boutique hotel. It is a low-lying building of glass and stone that is both a wonder of contemporary architecture and a perfect reflection of its primitive, traditional surroundings. The five private suites are a fine example of sumptuous simplicity, and the cooking … well, my very own mother-in-law Darina declared that the feast of sea urchins prepared by Ruairí was one of the best things she'd ever eaten. I could have stayed here for a week.

Satisfied and a little sad to leave, I return to the mainland and resume my exploration of Connemara. From Inverin I cut through the rusty bogs and lonely valleys of Connemara's interior. At Maam Cross I turn westward and, with the forebodingly beautiful Maumturk Mountains ahead of me, I get to Recess and one of my favourite spots in all of Ireland – the shimmering dark waters of Lough Inagh. On the western side are the moody Twelve Bens; the road along its eastern shore will take me north past wonderful Kylemore Abbey (originally built as a castle; now it's a well-respected girls' school) and onwards towards Connemara's northwestern tip.

In the fishing village of Cleggan I make sure that Johnny King's Western Kingfisher is moored in the boat-lined docks. Johnny runs angling trips, but he also catches fresh crab that he cooks right there in his shed – watching him prepare the crab is a masterclass in seafood preparation, and one that teaches me a lot. Mouth watering, I determine to get a takeaway crab salad or sandwich for the picnic I plan along one of the country's most scenic routes – the Sky Road.

The Sky Road is a 12km loop from Clifden out to the township of Kingston and back again. On a clear day, the views of Clifden Bay and its two offshore islands, Inishturk and Turbot, are spectacular, so I pull over and enjoy my crab sandwich in the ideal setting. About a kilometre out of Clifden is Monument Hill, which also has terrific views of the town as well as a stone memorial to John D'Arcy, who founded the town at the beginning of the 19th century.

All of this climbing and sightseeing has made me thirsty, and there's no better place around for a creamy pint than Guy's Bar & Snug, which as well as pulling a fine pint also serves delicious local seafood – crab salads, fishcakes, platters of fresh and smoked fish, and grilled fish. Now, when I'm in the need of a simple but stylish starter, I go to my Crab and blood orange salad (see page 240). Divine!

DETOUR: COASTAL ROAD TO CLIFDEN

The *other* way to get to Clifden is along the filigreed coastline west of Inverin. Instead of heading north I weave my way along the narrow roads that hug the water's edge. Carraroe (An Cheathrú Rua) peninsula has some gorgeous beaches and some wonderful personal memories: I went to Irish College here and still remember our various excursions to beautiful Coral Strand on Greatman's Bay! Alternatively, just to the north of Carraroe is the turn-off for the land bridge that links the islands of Lettermore, Gorumna and Lettermullen; bleak and beautiful spots populated by a small number of hardy farmers and fishermen. You can follow the coastline all the way around, past Carnaand on to Roundstone. About 3km beyond the village look for the turn to Gurteen Bay, one of the nicest beaches in the whole region; on the other side of the small peninsula is Dog's Bay, another gorgeous stretch of sand. A few kilometres further on, at Ballyconneely, is the Connemara Smokehouse where they've been smoking the region's freshly caught salmon, tuna and mackerel over beechwood since 1979. The family-run business offers a wide range of hand-filleted, traditionally smoked fish and even offers smokehouse tours to show you how it's done! If it's a bit of old-world charm you're after then I recommend a stay at the lovely Cashel House Hotel.

Whichever way I take to Clifden, I know that my final destination in Connemara is the magnificent estate at Ballynahinch Castle, where luxury and a traditional Irish welcome are comfortable bedfellows. The estate is renowned for many things – its beautiful bedrooms, the great restaurant, its wonderful walks … and its fly fishing. I'm no angler, but I'm keen to learn, and there are few better spots in Ireland to practise my casting than on the Ballynahinch River. Hopefully the lesson will result in something I can eat!

HOW TO COOK A CRAB

The meal of freshly cooked lobster with new potatoes, tomato and basil salad and cucumber pickle (see page 216) would be equally divine with freshly cooked crab in place of the lobster. Here's how to cook a crab, should you be lucky enough to get some live ones, as the meat will be all the more sweet and succulent if eaten as soon as it's cooked. Don't forget to scrape out the brown meat from the body – while it doesn't have the lovely flaky texture of the white meat from the claws, it does have a fantastic rich and salty flavour.

450g (1lb) of cooked crab in the shell yields 175–225g (6–8oz) crab meat

First, weigh the crab. Then place the crab in the freezer for two hours. Once the freezing time is up, remove the crabs from the freezer and place in a large saucepan, cover with measured warm water and add 1 tablespoon of salt for every 1.2 litres (2 pints) water. (The crab can be cooked in seawater but omit the salt). Bring to the boil, then turn the heat down and simmer on a medium heat for 20 minutes per 450g (1lb).

Pour off about two-thirds of the water, cover with a lid and continue to cook for a further 6 minutes. To check if the crab is cooked, use an oven glove or tea-towel to lift it out of the pan, then gently shake it quite close to your ear – you shouldn't hear liquid splashing around. Remove the crab and allow to cool.

When the crab has cooled, remove the large claws and crack these (using a heavy weight or nut crackers), then, using the handle of a tablespoon, extract every bit of meat. Retain the shell if you'd like it to serve the meat in, otherwise discard. Turn the body of the crab upside down and pull out the centre portion. Discard the gills, known as 'dead man's fingers' and each about 4cm (1½in) long. Scoop out all the lovely brown meat and add it to the white meat from the claws. The meat can be used immediately or frozen for future use.

CRAB AND BLOOD ORANGE SALAD

Serves 4–6 as a starter or light lunch

3 blood oranges (use regular when not in season)
400g (14oz) cooked crab meat
1 small red onion, peeled and thinly sliced
2 ripe avocados, halved, stone removed, peeled and cut into roughly 1cm (½in) dice
50ml (2fl oz) extra virgin olive oil, plus extra to serve
1 tbsp sherry vinegar
2 tbsp chopped dill (chopped coriander or parsley leaves also work well if you don't have dill)
salt and freshly ground black pepper
few handfuls of salad greens, to serve

First segment the oranges: cut a little slice from the top and bottom of the fruit. Next, stand the orange on a chopping board and, using a small sharp knife and following the curve of the orange, cut a strip of peel off from top to bottom. Continue around the orange until there is no peel remaining. Hold the orange over a bowl, then cut a segment out by slipping the knife in between one of the segments and the connective membrane. Cut down until you reach the middle of the orange, but don't cut through the membrane. Make another cut the other side of the segment against the other membrane and you will be left with a perfect segment, with no membrane. Repeat with the rest of the oranges, then squeeze the juice out from the pieces of peel and inner membrane over the segments in the bowl.

Add the crab meat, onion and avocado to the bowl and toss gently. Drizzle the olive oil and vinegar over, then add the chopped herbs and season with salt and pepper. Toss again, gently, so as not to break up the orange segments.

Place a small handful of salad greens on each plate, or all together on one large platter, drizzle with a little olive oil, then spoon the crab and blood orange salad over the top and serve.

BEER-BRAISED TURBOT WITH SAGE CREAM

Turbot is one of the really great fish; delicate in flavour yet firm in texture, it can be cooked successfully in any way. In this recipe I suggest cutting the fish down through the bones to give you steaks, rather than fillets, which brings lots of extra flavour from the bones and prevents the flesh breaking up.

Serves 4 as a main course

1 whole turbot, about 1.5kg (3¼lb)
50g (2oz) butter
4 shallots, peeled and finely chopped (125g/4½oz when chopped)
salt and freshly ground black pepper
50ml (2fl oz) white wine vinegar
400ml (14fl oz) beer, such as a wheat beer
200ml (7fl oz) hot fish stock
150ml (5fl oz) double or regular cream
2 tbsp chopped sage
1 tsp lemon juice

Cut the head off the turbot then, cutting down lengthways through the bones, cut the fish in half, then cut each half in two to make four steaks (tranches). Rinse with cold water, pat dry and set aside.

Place a wide (and shallow, if available) pan on a medium heat and melt the butter. When foaming, add the shallots and season with salt and pepper. Turn the heat down to low and cook, uncovered, for 5 minutes or until soft and very light golden, stirring regularly while cooking.

Add the vinegar and beer and bring to the boil, then boil on a high heat until the liquid is reduced to just a few tablespoons – be careful that it doesn't burn. Add the hot fish stock and lay the fish steaks in a single layer in the pan. Season with salt and pepper, cover and cook on a low–medium heat for 10–15 minutes, turning the fish over after 5 minutes, until cooked.

Lift the fish out of the pan, put on a plate and set aside somewhere warm if possible. Add the cream and sage to the pan and boil for a few seconds, then add the lemon juice and season with salt and pepper to taste.

To serve, remove the dark skin from the turbot. Put a little of the sauce on each warm plate, place the fish (still on the bone) on top, then drizzle generously with the sauce. Serve.

TURBOT ROAST WITH LEMON AND FENNEL

A delicious meal-in-one-dish; the turbot roasts beautifully on top of the lemons, surrounded by golden potato and onion wedges and the vegetable that all seafood adores – fennel.

Serves 4 as a main course

1 x 1.5kg (3¼lb) whole turbot
450g (1lb) potatoes, peeled and each cut into 6–8 wedges
2 large red onions, each peeled and cut into 8 wedges
2 large fennel bulbs, each trimmed (save the fronds for serving) and cut into
    8 wedges
50ml (2fl oz) extra virgin olive oil, plus 1 tsp for the fish
salt and freshly ground black pepper
1 lemon, cut into 8 wedges

Preheat the oven to 230°C (450°F), Gas mark 8.

Wash the turbot well, cleaning off any trace of blood. I like to leave the head on, but take it off if you wish (or ask your fishmonger to do this). Pat the fish dry and set aside.

Place the potato, onion and fennel wedges in a bowl. Drizzle with the 50ml (2fl oz) olive oil, season with salt and pepper and toss well. Tip into a roasting tin and place in the oven for 10 minutes.

Remove from the oven, push the vegetables to around the sides of the roasting tin and lay the lemon wedges in the centre. Sit the fish on top of the lemon, dark skin side up. Drizzle with the 1 teaspoon of olive oil and season with salt and pepper.

Place back in the oven and cook for a further 10–15 minutes until the fish and the vegetables are cooked.

CHARGRILLED SQUID WITH WARM SPICED SHERRY VINEGAR DRESSING

I've always adored the flavour and texture of squid. In this recipe it's not deep-fried, as it often is, but cooked on the hottest cast-iron griddle pan, to take on dark charred lines that will bring a gorgeous smokiness that's just perfect for the sherry vinegar dressing. Try it on the BBQ during summertime.

Serves 4–6 as a starter

2 cloves of garlic, peeled and crushed or finely grated
6 tbsp extra virgin olive oil
¼ tsp fine sea salt
few twists of freshly ground black pepper
1 tsp cumin seeds, toasted and ground (see page 149)
2 tsp coriander seeds, toasted and ground (see page 149)
½ tsp hot smoked paprika (or ¼ tsp sweet smoked paprika and ¼ tsp cayenne
    pepper)
300–350g (11–12oz) (3 small or 2 large) prepared squid tubes (weighed after
    head and intestines discarded – use tentacles and wings too, if you have them)
1 tbsp chopped coriander leaves
6 tsp sherry vinegar
a few coriander sprigs or rocket leaves, to serve

Put a griddle pan on the hob to heat up.

Mix the garlic, olive oil, salt, pepper and ground spices in a bowl and set aside.

Cut each squid (body and wings) into 4–6 equal pieces (I like to serve 2–3 pieces per person). Each piece will be about 6 x 8cm (2½ x 3¼in) in size. Score the outside of each piece into small diamonds, being careful not to cut all the way through. Rub the squid (including the tentacles) with a little of the spiced oil and set aside to marinate for a few minutes.

Mix the chopped coriander and vinegar with the rest of the spiced dressing.

Sear the squid on the very hot griddle pan for a minute or so on each side. Transfer to warm plates and drizzle with a little of the spiced dressing. Scatter a few coriander sprigs or rocket leaves over the top and serve.

IVAN'S CHINESE CRISPY MACKEREL PANCAKES

Another gem from Ivan, this recipe is up there at the top of my list of favourite things to eat. Much like the duck pancakes you get in Chinese restaurants (or indeed, China!), these are made with sustainable mackerel, which also happens to be stunningly good for you. Insanely good!

Serves 8–10 as a starter, or 4–6 as a main; makes 16–20 pancakes

8 fillets of mackerel, free from all bones, skin on
2 tsp soy sauce
2 tsp Chinese five-spice powder
16–20 Peking pancakes
2 tbsp hoisin sauce
2 tbsp oyster sauce
5 spring onions, trimmed and cut into matchstick-sized julienne
½ cucumber, cut into matchstick-sized julienne

FOR THE MARINADE
2 tsp sesame oil
2 tsp soy sauce
2 tsp Chinese five-spice powder

Mix all the ingredients for the marinade in a bowl and add the mackerel fillets, then turn them to ensure each fillet is well covered. Leave to marinate for 10–30 minutes, or a couple of hours would be great, but it's not essential.

Place the mackerel, flesh side down, in a cool frying pan, put on a medium heat and allow to come up to temperature and the oils can escape from the fish. Cook for 10 minutes or so until golden. Flip the fish over and break the flesh apart with your fish slice as it cooks. Sprinkle the soy and five-spice into the pan at this stage and fry for a further 10–15 minutes until the fish is golden and completely broken up into chunky pieces.

Preheat the oven to 170°C (325°F), Gas mark 3. Place the pancakes on a plate with a bowl over the top and warm in the oven. Mix the hoisin and oyster sauces with 2 tablespoons of water in a bowl.

Serve the stack of warm pancakes and a bowl of the warm cooked mackerel bits with the spring onions, cucumber and hoisin/oyster sauce mix. Allow people to make up their own pancakes and eat with their fingers.

CHINESE-STYLE STEAMED SEA BASS

When fish is steamed it stays amazingly moist and well able to soak up the wonderfully fragrant Chinese flavours in this recipe, one of my very favourites.

Serves 4–6 as a main course

¼ red chilli pepper, cut into very fine
    rings (seeds left in, if you wish)
2.5cm (1in) piece root ginger, peeled
    and cut into fine julienne strips
2 cloves of garlic, peeled and finely
    sliced
1 x 1.5kg (3lb 4oz) whole sea bass,
    gutted, cleaned and scaled
salt and freshly ground black pepper
25g (1oz) fresh coriander, leaves and
    small stalks chopped
50g (2oz) spring onions, trimmed and
    cut into julienne strips

juice of ½ lime
fluffy cooked rice, to serve

FOR THE DRESSING
1 tbsp toasted sesame oil
2 tbsp soy sauce (light Chinese soy,
    or Japanese)
2 tsp fish sauce
2 tbsp rice wine

You will need a big steamer for this recipe. Mix the chilli, ginger and garlic together, then place a third of it on a plate that fits into the steamer. Season the fish inside and out with salt and pepper, then place the fish on top of the flavourings. Put a further third of the flavourings into the fish cavity and scatter the rest over the top. Bring the water under the steamer to a boil, then carefully put the plate containing the fish into the steamer. Pop the lid on and time the fish for 12–15 minutes until just cooked in the centre.

Put all the ingredients for the dressing in a saucepan and heat.

Transfer the fish to a serving plate and sprinkle with the coriander and spring onion. Pour any cooking liquid left from the fish into the hot dressing, then pour this over the fish, spring onion and coriander. Finish with a squeeze of lime juice, and serve with fluffy rice.

RACHEL'S TIP
This recipe works perfectly well using a piece of fish, then scaling down the sauce and greens proportionally.

Alternatively, if you don't have a steamer, put two-thirds of the chilli, ginger and garlic into the cavity of the fish and top with the remaining third. Put into a roasting tin with a few tablespoons of water and cover tightly with foil. Put into a hot oven for 20–25 minutes until just cooked through, and then continue as above.

SQUID AND COCONUT BROTH

I love a Southeast Asian-style broth in any shape or form, and this deliciously flavoursome squid and noodle soup (which is not dissimilar to a laksa) is no exception. If you want to make it a more substantial meal, add some cooked rice noodles when serving.

Serves 4–6 as a starter

2 cloves of garlic, peeled
2cm (¾in) square piece of root ginger, peeled and roughly chopped
½ red chilli pepper (deseeded, if you wish)
50g (2oz) coriander, leaves and stalks, chopped
1 tbsp sunflower oil
1 x 400g tin of coconut milk
200g (7oz) prepared squid tubes (weighed after head and intestines discarded),
    opened out and cut into very thin 0.5 x 2cm (¼ x ¾in) slices
juice of 1 lime
2½–3 tbsp Thai or Vietnamese fish sauce
2 large handfuls of shredded Chinese greens or iceberg lettuce
1 tbsp each of thinly sliced spring onion, basil and mint leaves, mixed together

Place the garlic, ginger, chilli and coriander in a small food processor and whiz until you have an almost fine green paste. Add the sunflower oil and whiz again for a few seconds.

Place a saucepan on a medium–high heat and tip in the coriander paste. Cook for just a few seconds until hot, then add the coconut milk and 250ml (9fl oz) water. Bring to the boil, tip in the squid and cook for just half a minute. Take off the heat and add the lime juice and fish sauce to taste. You can add more if necessary.

Place your warm bowls on the work surface and add some shredded greens or lettuce to each, then divide the broth among the bowls.

Scatter with the spring onion, basil and mint mixture and serve.

IRISH SWEET AND SOUR HONEY-GLAZED SPATCHCOCK DUCK

I'm a big fan of the spatchcocked bird. With the simple process of just cutting down the backbone and spreading the bird out, the legs and breast cook perfectly evenly and the slightly flattened shape lends itself well to adding myriad ingredients. In this recipe I use the delightful sweet and sour flavours that go so well with the rich duck meat.

Serves 4–6 as a main course

1 duck
salt and freshly ground black pepper
50g (2oz) butter
600g (1lb 6oz) shallots, peeled and halved through the core
4 tbsp honey
4 tbsp cider vinegar
4 tsp whole thyme leaves (not chopped)

Preheat the oven to 150°C (300°F), Gas mark 2.

Hold the duck upright and, using strong scissors or a chopping knife, split it down its backbone and open it out. Pull out any excess lumps of fat. (Keep these and put them in a small ovenproof bowl in the oven to render/melt down, then pour into a jar, cool and store in the fridge for cooking roast potatoes.)

Place the duck, skin side up, on a wire rack set in a deep roasting tin. Score the skin in a criss-cross fashion, then sprinkle with salt and pepper. Put the duck into the oven and roast for 2–2½ hours until a leg pulls away easily from the body.

While the duck is roasting, melt the butter in a sauté pan or frying pan that will hold the shallots in one layer and add salt and pepper. Add the shallots to the pan and fry gently on a medium heat until golden on all sides and just tender. Add the honey, cider vinegar and thyme leaves and allow to bubble for a few minutes. Using a slotted spoon, remove the shallots from the pan, leaving the glaze behind. Place the shallots in an ovenproof gratin dish big enough to also hold the duck.

When the duck is cooked, carefully remove the tray from the oven – it will be full of fat. Pour off all the fat into the same jar in which you stored the duck fat earlier. Increase the oven temperature to 230°C (450°F), Gas mark 8.

Place the duck on top of the shallots and spoon the glaze over the skin of the duck, covering all of it. Return to the oven for 10–15 minutes and cook until the shallots are a deep golden brown.

APPLE CUSTARD FOOL

Light fluffy apple stirred through sweet vanilla-scented custard and served with crumbly, buttery shortbread biscuits. A deliciously comforting autumnal pudding, this is a perfect way to end a Sunday lunch.

Serves 4

2 x 185g (6½oz) eating apples, peeled, cored and quartered
3–4 sweet geranium or lemon verbena leaves (optional)
150ml (5fl oz) milk
1 large or 2 small egg yolks
50g (2oz) caster sugar
15g (½oz) plain flour
1 tsp vanilla extract
juice of ½ lemon
75ml (3fl oz) double or regular cream, softly whipped
shortbread biscuits, to serve

Chop the apples into 2–3cm (¾–1¼in) chunks and place in a small saucepan with 4 tablespoons of water. I love to put 3–4 sweet geranium or lemon verbena leaves into the apple while they cook, for even more flavour. Put on a medium heat and bring the water to the boil, then cover with a lid, turn the heat down to low and cook the apples for about 15 minutes until completely softened. Set aside to cool.

While the apples are cooling, pour the milk into a saucepan and bring to the boil, then take off the heat. Place the egg yolk(s) in a heatproof bowl with the sugar, flour and vanilla extract and whisk together. Pour the warm milk into the bowl while whisking, then pour this mixture back into the saucepan on a medium heat and whisk the mixture as it comes to the boil. Watch out – as soon as it boils it will go lumpy, so keep whisking. Once it is thick, take it off the heat, tip into a bowl and allow to cool.

Mash the cooked apple, add the lemon juice and fold together with the cooled custard and softly whipped cream. Serve with shortbread biscuits.

RACHEL'S TIP
You only need the egg yolk(s) for this recipe. Store the egg white(s) in the fridge for up to 2 weeks for making meringues.

Ballycroy National Park –
one of Europe's largest blanket
bogs. It is here, in the wild
and beautiful expanse of north
Mayo, that the herbs, blossoms
and berries grow.

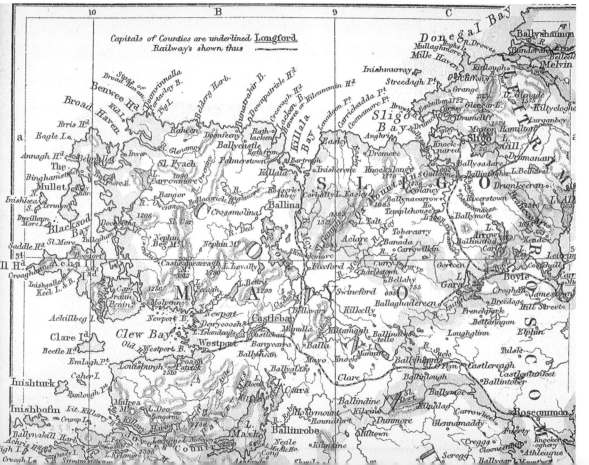

MAYO

CLARE ISLAND AND SLIGO

MAYO, CLARE ISLAND AND SLIGO

I bid farewell to Connemara along its northern coast, skirting the southern side of the beautiful Killary fjord, but the goodbye isn't too sad because I know that on the other side of the inlet is County Mayo, whose wild beauty reminds me of where I've just come from. At Leenane I head north for Westport, and looming majestically ahead of me as I drive is the sacred peak of Croagh Patrick, Ireland's holiest mountain.

DETOUR: DOOLOUGH VALLEY

An alternative route from Leenane to Westport is the 54km drive via through the desolate Doolough Valley, one of the country's most beautiful scenic routes. The road skirts along the eastern edge of the Doo Lough, the steep sides of the surrounding mountains sliding quietly into the dark waters of the lough; there's ne'er a trace of life around these parts except sheep grazing on the hillsides, which makes the drive all that more beautiful. The side roads north and west of the valley lead to some beautiful, usually deserted beaches.

The route is also a part of Ireland's poignant history: it was here in the cold winter of 1849, during the Famine, that 400 people died of starvation and exhaustion on a desperate march to Delphi to ask their landlords for help.

On a clear day, the Reek (as the mountain is also known) is the ideal vantage point from which to look over all of Clew Bay and its 365 (or so I'm told!) islands. The truly penitent like to climb it in bare feet, replicating the feat of St Patrick himself, who, legend has it, fasted for 40 days and nights atop its stony peak.

In its shadow is the Georgian town of Westport, one of my favourite towns in Ireland. I choose to eat at the recently opened and absolutely stunning The Idle Wall. Situated just outside the black gates of Westport House, this restaurant serves wonderful food and is well worth a stop.

Afterwards I pop my head into Matt Molloy's, the famous pub opened by and named after the Chieftains' fife player. It's one of the best places in the whole county to catch some live music.

Westport is also a great spot to get on the Great Western Greenway, a 42km cycling trail that follows the old Wesport–Achill railway line. It's divided into three sections; the middle bit, the 18km cycle between Newport and Mulranny, is the most popular as its skirts the edge of Clew Bay.

DETOUR: CLARE ISLAND

The biggest of Clew Bay's islands is Clare Island, which you can get to by ferry from Louisburgh. This was the home of the fearsome 16th-century pirate queen, Granuaile, who resisted everything and anyone – including the English – who would dare attempt to take her ancestral lands from her. These days, Clare is a great spot to go walking, and the old lighthouse (built in 1806) is now a gorgeous boutique hotel with elegant rooms and a really good restaurant, serving a six-course dinner menu of local seafood and meats as well as homemade preserves and chutneys and artisan cheeses.

I drive north alongside the greenway and take a nice detour along the Atlantic Way, which runs clockwise around the Curraun Peninsula on Clew Bay's northern shores. There are some old fortified towers along here, but the views back across the bay are the real attraction – I pause on my route, to take a moment to remind myself how beautiful Ireland truly is.

I proceed north-west, through the broad expanse of Ballycroy National Park, one of Europe's largest blanket bogs. It is here, in the wild and beautiful expanse of north Mayo, that the herbs, blossoms and berries grow that are used to make the award-winning Wildwood Vinegars (Lissadrone, Carrowmore-Lacken, Ballina) just north of Ballina. The vinegars, which come in 100ml and 200ml sizes, are a delicious variety of balsamics – blackberry, raspberry and elderflower. Or if you prefer there are regular vinegars, with intoxicating names like Wild Rose Petal, Wild Mountain Thyme and Wild Garlic and Samphire. In every mouthful you can taste the landscape; close your eyes, savour the taste and you are back in the wilds of north Mayo. I buy a selection of each, and when my tour is over I immortalise this part of my trip in a Venison and red wine stew (see page 268) infused with one of their balsamics.

It's late afternoon now, and as I cross the border into County Sligo the sun begins to set. I make my way to the small village of Drumcliff, where in the small churchyard is buried Nobel laureate W.B. Yeats. He picked the setting himself – in the shadow of Sligo's most famous peak, Ben Bulben – and carefully selected his own epitaph, from his poem *Under Ben Bulben:* Cast a cold eye / On life, on death / Horseman, pass by!

I head through Sligo Town, stopping to try a famous homemade gelato at Fabio's. The range is incredible, and as soon as I'm home I feel I have to try out different ice cream recipes – the winner being Honey and mint buttermilk (see page 272). Delicious! Then it's off to Strandhill, where I wear off the cares of the day with a deeply satisfying seaweed bath at Voya – ah, bliss. I follow it with some lunch at Shell's Café & Little Shop right on the seafront

– all their breads are baked in-house, and they endeavour to use only the best local produce…and the proof is in the pudding (they do a lovely chocolate cake). Tucking into their delicious cakes gave me the idea for my Pear and gingerbread crumble (see page 274) – a favourite of mine for teatime. I'm a little spoilt for choice when it comes to where to stay, as Sligo has a handful of truly exceptional places with plenty of style and character. Coopershill, about 25km south of Sligo Town, is a luxurious country manor with six beautiful rooms with enticing names – Georgian, Pink, School and Venetian … the last one is the original master bedroom and has *two* four-poster beds in it!

Roughly the same distance south of Sligo Town is another luxury house with plenty of character. You'll meander up a half-mile road through private parkland to reach Temple House, which is a historic home offering bed and a delicious, hearty breakfast and lovely rooms. The grounds are perfect for a walk after a long day's driving, with even a 13th-century castle on the grounds, so I stretch my legs and feel the evening breeze.

RED MULLET WITH LEMON OIL AND GRILLED ASPARAGUS

A quick, easy, late spring–early summer dish, perfect for when asparagus is in season. Use a really good extra virgin olive oil.

Serves 4 as a main course

grated zest and juice of 1 lemon
50ml (2fl oz) extra virgin olive oil
salt and freshly ground black pepper
12–16 stalks of asparagus, woody ends snapped off and discarded, cut ends
    trimmed and peeled
4 x 175g (6oz) fillets of red mullet, scaled

Combine the lemon zest and the olive oil in a little bowl or cup.

Bring a large pan of water to the boil and pop a large griddle pan on a high heat on the hob to heat. When the water is boiling, add a large pinch of salt, drop in the asparagus and boil, uncovered, for 2½ minutes, then remove. Drain, then plunge the asparagus into cold water to refresh. Drain again and dry on a clean tea towel or kitchen paper.

Toss the asparagus in the hot griddle pan and drizzle a little lemon oil over it. Turn the stalks so they char slightly on all sides. Set aside and keep warm.

Bring the griddle pan back to a high heat. Season the fish fillets, score the skin and rub with the remaining lemon oil. Cook the fish, flesh side down, in the pan until golden brown, then turn them over to cook the other side. It should take just a minute or two on either side to cook if the pan is good and hot.

Divide the asparagus among four hot plates, squeeze juice from the lemon over the fish while still in the pan, then place the fillets on the asparagus and serve.

MUSSELS WITH STAR ANISE, CHERVIL AND CREAM

This is a gorgeous recipe that my cousin-in-law Ivan makes regularly. It takes only a few minutes to whip up, making it an ideal, convenient starter or main course. Thankfully, we have an abundance of deliciously sweet mussels in Ireland and they're good value, too.

Serves 4 as a starter, or 2 as a main course, with crusty bread

1kg (2lb 2oz) mussels in their shells, well washed and cleaned – discard any that are not tightly shut or don't close when tapped
100ml (3½fl oz) cider (the drier the better)
100ml (3½fl oz) double or regular cream
2 star anise
2 generous tbsp chopped chervil

Place a wide saucepan (one that will easily hold all the mussels when they've opened) on a high heat. When it is hot, add all the ingredients at the same time and cover the pan.

Toss the mussels around in the pan occasionally for 4–5 minutes, until all the mussels are open and the sauce has slightly thickened. Discard any mussels that remain closed.

Serve immediately in warm bowls.

VENISON AND RED WINE STEW

A beautifully rich and wintery stew that's given a fresh burst of flavour by the balsamic vinegar and red currant jelly at the end of cooking. This is just as delicious, if not more so, made a day before serving. It's also a great one for the freezer.

Serves 6 as a main course

600g (1lb 6oz) stewing venison, trimmed and cut into 2–3cm (¾–1¼in) chunks

40g (1½oz) plain flour

salt and freshly ground black pepper

2–4 tbsp extra virgin olive oil

250g (9oz) back bacon, cut into 1cm (½in) lardons

350g (12oz) onion, peeled and chopped into 1–2cm (½–¾in) chunks

2 cloves of garlic, peeled and chopped

300g (11oz) carrots, cut into 2cm (¾in) chunks

175ml (6fl oz) red wine

550ml (19fl oz) chicken or venison stock

3 tbsp tomato purée

150g (5oz) wild mushrooms

3 tbsp balsamic vinegar

3 tbsp redcurrant jelly

Preheat the oven to 150°C (300°F), Gas mark 2. Toss the venison in the flour with a good pinch of salt and pepper.

Heat 2 tablespoons of the olive oil in a large flameproof casserole or ovenproof saucepan. Fry the bacon in the olive oil on a medium–high heat until golden, then transfer to a plate, leaving the oil behind. Fry the venison in the pan until browned on all sides, being careful not to burn it. Add a little more olive oil if necessary.

Remove the venison, then add the onion, garlic and carrot and cook for a few minutes until slightly golden. Add the wine, stock and tomato purée and bring to the boil, stirring to remove any lumps. Return the venison to the pan, cover, and place in the oven for 2–2½ hours until the venison is tender.

While the venison is cooking, heat a frying pan on a high heat. Add in a drizzle of olive oil, then sauté the wild mushrooms until soft and golden, seasoning with salt and pepper.

When the venison is cooked, take it out of the oven and stir in the mushrooms with the balsamic vinegar and redcurrant jelly.

Serve with creamy mash or a baked spud. It's even better served the next day.

RAW CUCUMBER SOUP

A deliciously healthy way to start a summer meal, this is one of the fastest recipes there is. Keep chilled in the fridge (for up to 4 hours) until you're ready to serve.

Serves 4 as a starter

FOR THE SOUP
70g (2¾oz) celery, trimmed and very finely chopped
250g (9oz) cucumber, chopped
finely grated zest and juice of 1 lemon
good pinch of salt
good twist of black pepper
150g (5oz) natural yoghurt
1–2 tsp finely grated horseradish

TO FINISH
250g (9oz) grated cucumber
2 tsp chopped parsley leaves
2 tsp chopped coriander leaves
1 spring onion, trimmed and very finely chopped

Put all the soup ingredients into a blender and whiz to a smooth liquid. Pour into a bowl, add all the remaining ingredients, then cover and chill.

Before you serve, check the seasoning. Serve in small bowls with crusty bread as a gorgeous starter on a hot sunny day.

HONEY AND MINT BUTTERMILK ICE CREAM

This recipe was given to me by a past student and Ballymaloe friend, Jared Batson. The tart buttermilk balances beautifully with the sweet honey and fresh mint.

Serves 4

4 egg yolks
85g (3¼oz) caster or granulated sugar
4 full-leafed sprigs of fresh mint, plus extra to serve
225ml (8fl oz) double or regular cream
85g (3¼oz) honey
225ml (8fl oz) buttermilk
pinch of salt

In a bowl and using an electric whisk, whisk the egg yolks with 35g (scant 1½oz) of the sugar until the mixture is thick and mousse-like.

Remove the leaves from the mint sprigs and roughly chop. Place the cream, honey and remaining sugar in a saucepan on a medium heat with the chopped mint and stir until the sugar and honey are fully dissolved and the cream just begins to ever-so-gently boil. This is called the shivery stage, as the surface of the mixture looks like it's slightly 'shivering'.

Once the cream is ready, slowly pour it into the egg yolk and sugar mixture, whisking as you pour.

Return the mixture to the saucepan and cook slowly on a low heat, stirring all the time, making sure it doesn't get too hot and scramble. You might need to take it off the heat every so often if you think it's heating up too much. When the mixture becomes thick and coats the back of a wooden spoon, remove, pour through a sieve and leave to cool.

Once cool, whisk in the buttermilk and salt. Pour into an ice-cream machine and blend until thick and smooth, then freeze in a freezerproof container.

Serve with a chiffonade (very thinly sliced) of fresh mint over the top.

PEAR AND GINGERBREAD CRUMBLE

Of course it's no secret that pears loves a bit of spice, and if you find yourself in the fortunate position of having a little bit of leftover gingerbread, then can I recommend this delicious comforting crumble? It works just as well with apples.

Serves 6

6–8 pears (900g/2lb total weight), peeled, quartered and cored
110g (3¾oz) caster sugar

FOR THE CRUMBLE
200g (7oz) gingerbread (see page 276 for recipe)
75g (3oz) oat flakes
75g (3oz) unsalted butter, melted

Preheat the oven to 180°C (350°F), Gas mark 4.

Cut the pears into chunks 2–3cm (¾–1¼in) in size and place in a saucepan with 50ml (2fl oz) water and the sugar. Cover with a lid, place on a low heat and cook for 8–10 minutes until the pear is soft. Tip into a 1 litre (1¾ pint) capacity pie dish (or 6 individual ramekins).

To make the crumble, break the gingerbread up into crumbs, leaving it slightly coarse. Mix in a bowl with the oat flakes and melted butter, then pour over the pear mixture so that it's coating the pears evenly. Bake in the oven for 30–40 minutes until slightly crunchy on top. (Individual ramekins will take 15–20 minutes.)

Serve with softly whipped cream or custard.

IRISH GINGERBREAD

I can't remember the first time I ate a slice of gingerbread; it's always been something I've adored, and particularly so with great butter spread over the slice, and a cup of tea on the side. One of my favourite treats for a mid-afternoon catch up, this happily keeps for a week in a tin or airtight box.

Makes 1 loaf

60g (2½oz) unsalted butter
75g (3oz) treacle
50g (2oz) golden syrup
140g (4¾oz) plain flour
1 tsp bicarbonate of soda
½ tsp baking powder
2 tsp ground ginger
1 tsp ground cinnamon
1 tsp freshly grated nutmeg

100g (3½oz) caster sugar
pinch of salt
1 egg
125ml (4½fl oz) milk

FOR THE SYRUP
75g (3oz) caster sugar
2 tsp finely grated root ginger, or
    finely chopped crystallised ginger

Preheat the oven to 170°C (325°F), Gas mark 3. Line the base and sides of a 900g (2lb) loaf tin with baking parchment.

Melt the butter, treacle and golden syrup in a small saucepan on a low heat, then set aside.

Sift the flour, bicarbonate of soda and baking powder into a bowl and stir in the spices, sugar and salt. In another bowl, whisk the egg, then add the milk and the melted butter mixture and pour into the dry ingredients. Mix until smooth – it will have a wet, sloppy consistency.

Pour into the prepared loaf tin and bake in the oven for 50–55 minutes until risen and firm to the touch and a skewer inserted into the centre comes out clean. (Wait for at least 45 minutes before opening the oven to check whether the gingerbread has cooked, otherwise it can collapse in the centre.)

While the gingerbread is cooking, make the syrup. Place the sugar and ginger in a small saucepan with 75ml (3fl oz) water, bring to the boil on a medium heat and boil, uncovered, for 5 minutes or until slightly thickened and syrupy.

Once the gingerbread is cooked, take it out of the oven and, leaving it in the tin, pierce it all over the top with a fine skewer, then pour the syrup over and leave to cool completely.

When the gingerbread is cold, take it out of the tin and serve.

HOW TO MAKE AN IRISH COFFEE

It's said that the first Irish coffee was created by Joe Sheridan, who was the chef in the airport at Foynes, County Limerick, from where the Flying Boats used to head out to America. One very stormy night in 1942 the pilot, who had just left Irish land, had to admit defeat and turn back because of the bad weather, so chef Joe had the job of feeding the exhausted and understandably quite shaken travellers – hence the strong and soothing concoction of coffee, cream, sugar and Irish whiskey.

In the original recipe Joe calls for cream rich as an Irish brogue, coffee strong as a friendly hand, sugar sweet as the tongue of a rogue and whiskey smooth as the wit of the land.

The story of Irish Coffee is commemorated in the Flying Boat Museum at Foynes.

Serves 1

150ml (5fl oz) delicious hot coffee
2 tsp brown sugar
1 measure (35.5ml/generous 1¼fl oz) of Irish whiskey
50ml (2fl oz) double or whipping cream, very softly whipped

Pour the coffee into a heatproof glass. Stir in the sugar and whiskey.

Fill a jug or cup with boiling water and put a tablespoon into it for a few seconds. Take the spoon out of the hot water and immediately spoon the cream gently over the coffee. Dip the spoon back into the boiling water and repeat until you have 1.5–2cm (⅝–¾in) of softly whipped cream sitting on top of the coffee. Serve immediately.

The further north you go in
Donegal the more dramatic
the scenery becomes. Beyond
Dungloe is the rocky Rosses, an
Irish-speaking area punctured
with dark lakes and granite
cliffs, their dark, brooding
beauty every now and again
lightened by coves of glittering
golden sand.

COUNTY DONEGAL

CO. DONEGAL

COUNTY DONEGAL

I'm nearly at the end of my journey along the wild Atlantic coast. My last destination is wondrous, wild Donegal, tucked into Ireland's northwestern corner. It's the only county in Ireland without a rail link, which makes it that bit harder to get to, but there's all the more reason to try: dramatic coastlines and dark, brooding interiors make Donegal a scenic wonderland.

My first stop is along the shores of Lough Eske, just north of Donegal Town. Here are two of Ireland's finest hotels, Lough Eske Castle and, a little further on, Harvey's Point, both of which exude luxury and exquisite service, not to mention fabulous views of the lough!

But I've a lot of exploring to do before I settle in for the night. I head west, making a short stop in Mountcharles. Not only is there a beautiful sandy beach about 2km south of town, but I want to check out the green pump at the top of the village that in the 1940s and 50s was where native poet Séamus MacManus practised the ancient art of the *seanachaí*, or storyteller. Here he told fantastical tales of fairies, spirits and mythological battles to all who would come to listen. I sit and imagine the scene, looking around me at the village as it goes about its business.

The sea cliffs at Slieve League don't get half the fanfare of the Cliffs of Moher, but they're taller (at 600m they're amoung the tallest in Europe) and, on a wild day, just as dramatic. A great way to see them is from the sea itself, aboard the *Nuala Star Teelin*, bobbing up and down through the waves and taking in their sheer height and splendour from underneath the soaring rocks.

At the tip of the peninsula is the early Christian monastery of Glencolumbcille, founded in the 6th century by St Columba among a cluster of Stone Age standing stones that are evidence of a settlement here as far back as 3000 BC.

A more recent traditional way of life is immortalised in Father McDyer's Folk Village, about 3km away by the beach. Among the old thatched cottages is a craft shop that sells wines made from local plants (like seaweed and fuchsia) and homemade chocolates, butterscotches, marmalades and jams. An idyllic spot to sample foodie treasures.

I leave Glencolumbcille with a box of goodies and set off along a narrow rural route that brings me through the stunning Glen Gesh Pass – it's a little slice of the Alps in Ireland, so I open the car window and let in the fresh mountain air. On the far side is the lovely craft village of Ardara, the homeland of Donegal's woollen and tweed industry. I visit the local heritage centre and stop for lunch in Nancy's Bar, where I'm served an excellent seafood chowder in what seems like the family's sitting room!

The further north you go in Donegal the more dramatic the scenery becomes.

Beyond Dungloe is the rocky Rosses, an Irish-speaking area punctured with dark lakes and granite cliffs, their dark, brooding beauty every now and again lightened by coves of glittering golden sand.

DETOUR: THE POISONED GLEN

Inland to the east is the Poisoned Glen, a rocky valley that makes for a stunning, 4km circular walk. At the bottom of the valley is Dunlewey and its ruined church, where you will find the beginning of the trail. According to legend, the name came from the poison that Lugaidh used to kill his grandfather, the one-eyed king Balor; but the real story is more accidental. An English cartographer misspelt the name given it by the locals – An Gleann Neamhe (the Heavenly Glen) – as An Gleann Neimhe, the poisoned glen!

Further along the coast, Dunfanaghy is one of northwestern Donegal's most appealing towns, spread out along the broad crescent of Killahoey Beach beneath bulbous Horn Head. For dining, I'm spoilt for choice between the Cove and its fine selection of seafood and fish dishes, including an excellent chowder and fresh local crab and lobster, and The Mill, an elegant restaurant inside an old flax mill that serves local seafood with a modern Irish twist. The taste of the lobster fresh from the sea inspired me to cook lobster back at home – so simple yet so delicious.

On the far side of Sheephaven Bay, high in the hills of the Rosguill Peninsula, is another wonderful trove of dining goodness. Tucked in behind the traditional, dip-your-head-as-you-go-in-the-door Olde Glen Bar is a farmhouse restaurant that specialises in seafood but serves up other popular pub dishes, such as steak. You'll have to show up early to be guaranteed a table, but you can always have a pint in the bar at the front while you wait!

The countryside here is simply stunning. Getting lost on the small country roads is all part of the experience, and is a happy accident, because no matter where you go you'll find a beautiful view, a shimmering lake or the glimpse of golden sand.

There's a marvellous circular loop around the Inishowen Peninsula, past ancient sites, crumbling castles and the odd thatched cottage. At the tip is Ireland's northernmost point, Malin Head, and there are days when the only other life you'll share the views with are the birds, 200 species of which like to make the headland their temporary, migratory home. It is worth a stop to sit and hear the almost total silence, punctuated only by the sound of sea birds.

But my final stop on this epic journey is the peninsula just to the west. At the foot of Fanad Peninsula is the fine heritage town of Rathmelton, lined with

Georgian houses and stone-walled warehouses against the banks of the River Lennon. I'm here to try the seafood restaurant on the first floor of the Bridge Bar, one of the best in the county, and it doesn't disappoint. If I want to eat in a beautiful old country house where I can also lay my weary head then I have a couple of choices. I could head straight for Castle Grove House where I will receive the warmest of welcomes from Mary and Irene Sweeney and their team. Or I could head down the road to Rathmullan House, and it is here, amid the luxurious surroundings of this gorgeous 19th-century manor home, that I finally come to the end of the road. I retreat to my room with a deep sense of satisfaction at the experiences I've had and the stunning beauty of the Wild Atlantic coast; all that's left for me now is to sleep … and to plot my way home again!

GRILLED SALMON WITH TOMATO, OLIVE AND ROCKET SALSA

A lovely summertime recipe, the sharp, intense flavours of the salsa work a treat with rich, oily salmon. This is also great using mackerel in place of the salmon.

Serves 4 as a main course

4 x 150–185g (5–6½oz) salmon fillets, skin on but scaled
1 tbsp extra virgin olive oil
salt and freshly ground black pepper

FOR THE TOMATO, OLIVE AND ROCKET SALSA
3 ripe tomatoes, or 12 ripe cherry tomatoes, chopped into 1cm (½in) dice
12 good black olives, pitted and coarsely chopped
½ red onion, peeled and chopped
60g (2½oz) rocket leaves
75ml (3fl oz) extra virgin olive oil
juice of ½ lemon
good pinch of salt
pinch of sugar
twist of black pepper

Rub the salmon fillets with the tablespoon of olive oil, season with salt and pepper and set aside.

Combine all the ingredients for the salsa in a bowl and set aside.

Heat a grill pan on the hob and heat the grill of your oven at the same time. When the pan is very hot, add the salmon, flesh side down, and cook on the hob for about 2 minutes. Do not turn the fish over. Put the pan of fish into the oven close to the top, under the grill. Cook for a further 5–8 minutes, depending on how you like your fish cooked.

Place some salsa on each plate, then top with a salmon fillet and scatter with more salsa and serve.

PAN-FRIED GURNARD WITH LEMON AND SAFFRON BUTTER

The colourful gurnard is a gorgeous fish with a lovely meaty flesh; it's good value to buy and thankfully there are plenty of them about. I adore this perfumed saffron and lemon butter sauce, which by the way also goes well with monkfish or John Dory.

Serves 3 as a main course

3 x 350g (12oz) medium gurnard, filleted (60–70g/2½–2¾oz each fillet), to give
  2 fillets per person
30g (1¼oz) soft butter
salt and freshly ground black pepper

FOR THE LEMON AND SAFFRON BUTTER
pinch of sugar
pinch of saffron threads
2 tbsp hot water
juice of ½ lemon (about 2 tbsp)
60g (2½oz) butter

Put the sugar, saffron and hot water in a small bowl or cup and leave to infuse.

Rub the fish fillets on both sides with the soft butter and season with salt and pepper. Place the fish, flesh side down, in a hot pan and fry until golden brown, then flip it over and fry the skin side. Transfer to warm plates.

Put the water and saffron mix, the lemon juice and butter into the pan the fish was cooked in and heat until bubbling and reduced to the consistency of cream.

Spoon the lemon and saffron butter over the fillets and serve immediately with a green salad.

FISH GRATIN WITH LEEKS

I do like a one-pot meal and this lovely simple gratin recipe is just perfect for a Sunday roast or mid-week supper.

Serves 4–6 as a main course

30g (1¼oz) butter

2 medium leeks (650g/1lb 7oz total weight, or 425g/15oz when trimmed), trimmed, washed, halved lengthways and cut at an angle into 7.5cm (3in) slices

salt and freshly ground black pepper

1kg (2lb 2oz) potatoes (weighed with skins), peeled (800g/1¾lb after peeling)

300ml (11fl oz) milk

250ml (9fl oz) double or regular cream

1 clove of garlic, peeled and crushed

small pinch of freshly grated nutmeg

1 large sprig of fresh thyme, leaves picked off, stalk discarded

1 bay leaf

650g (1lb 7oz) filleted and skinned round white fish, such as cod, pollock, hake (this is about a 1.5kg/3¼lb fish with head on)

75g (3oz) Cheddar cheese, grated

Preheat the oven to 170°C (325°F), Gas mark 3.

Melt the butter in a saucepan on a medium heat, add the leeks, 1 tablespoon of water and some salt and pepper to season. Turn the heat down to low, cover and cook for 3 minutes or until the leeks are just soft. Take off the heat and lay out in a 2 litre (3½ pint) gratin dish.

Next, place the potato slices in the empty saucepan and add the milk, cream, garlic, nutmeg and herbs with some salt and pepper. Bring to the boil, then cover the pan, turn the heat down and simmer for 5 minutes, stirring gently every minute. Be very careful that the mixture doesn't stick.

While the potatoes are cooking, lay the fish over the leeks to cover completely and season with salt and pepper.

When the potatoes are cooked, take them off the heat (if you want to prepare this in advance, cool the potatoes before placing them over the fish). Arrange the potatoes and all the sauce over the fish, then scatter with the grated cheese. Cook in the oven for 50 minutes or until golden, bubbling and the potatoes are cooked. If it is golden after 40 minutes but the potatoes are not yet soft, cover with a sheet of baking parchment and continue to cook. Serve with a delicious green salad.

OXTAIL AND WHITE BEAN CASSEROLE WITH SALSA VERDE

This is the kind of meal that I long for on cold winter evenings. For a seriously succulent result, do make sure to give the oxtail plenty of time to cook. The salsa verde also happens to be great with every other meat I can think of, and fish too.

Serves 4 as a main course

240g (8½oz) dried white cannellini or haricot beans, soaked in cold water, to cover, overnight, or 2 x 400g tins of cannellini or haricot beans, strained and liquid reserved
1–2 tbsp olive oil
1.25kg (2¾lb) oxtail (1 large oxtail), cut into 4–6cm (1½–2½in) pieces
salt and freshly ground black pepper
1 large red onion, peeled and sliced
2 large cloves of garlic, peeled and crushed or finely grated
800g (1¾lb) fresh, ripe tomatoes, peeled and chopped, or 2 x 400g tins of chopped tomatoes
2 sprigs of fresh rosemary
pinch of sugar

FOR THE SALSA VERDE (MAKES 150ML/5FL OZ)
1 good handful of flat-leaf parsley leaves
grated zest and juice of 1 small lemon
2 cloves of garlic, peeled and crushed
1 tbsp capers, rinsed
50ml (2fl oz) olive oil

Drain the soaked beans, put in a saucepan and cover with cold water. Place on a high heat and bring to the boil, then boil until softened, 45–60 minutes. When cooked, strain the beans, reserving the cooking water. If using tinned beans, strain those, too, saving the liquid in the tin.

Preheat the oven to 150°C (300°F), Gas mark 2.

Place a flameproof casserole or saucepan on a high heat and add 1 tablespoon of olive oil. When hot, add the oxtail pieces and brown them on all sides, seasoning with salt and pepper. Take the oxtail pieces out of the pan and set aside.

Keep the pan on the heat and turn the heat down to low. Tip in the onion and garlic and add a further tablespoon of olive oil if there isn't any fat left in the pan

from the oxtail. Season with salt and pepper, cover the pan and cook the onions for 5 minutes or until softened. Add the tomatoes and rosemary with a good pinch of sugar. Bring to the boil, then stir in the beans with 150ml (5fl oz) of the cooking water (or the liquid in the tins) and the browned oxtail pieces. Stir on the heat for 1 minute, then cover with a lid, place in the oven and cook for 2½–3 hours until the meat is almost falling off the bone.

Meanwhile, make the salsa verde. Put the parsley, lemon zest, garlic and capers in a food processor and whiz until it's all finely chopped. Add the lemon juice and olive oil (adding more oil if you want it a bit more runny). Check the seasoning – it might not need salt, as the capers can be quite salty, but add a twist of pepper. If not using straightaway, tip into a jar and cover with 5mm (¼in) of olive oil, then place in the fridge, where it will keep for up to 3 weeks.

Serve the oxtail with some salsa verde drizzled over the top.

HOW TO MAKE CELERY SALT

I can't taste celery salt without thinking of my time living in Vancouver in the mid 1990s, where Bloody Caesars were the thing to drink at Sunday brunch. It is just like a Bloody Mary but made with clamato juice (which has clam juice in it) instead of tomato juice, and finished with a good dusting of celery salt. This will transform your Bloody Mary forever.

Celery salt is also great for seasoning lamb, pork, chicken or root vegetables, and makes a lovely seasoning for fish. Cumin salt can be made in the same way.

Place equal quantities of celery seeds and salt (1 tsp of each or 1 tbsp of each) into a pestle and mortar and grind together.

CARPACCIO OF JERUSALEM ARTICHOKE WITH ROASTED HAZELNUTS, AVOCADO AND WATERCRESS

Carpaccio gets its name from the dish of thinly sliced raw beef that echoes the white and red colours often used by the 15th-century Venetian artist of the same name. This delicious dish takes the thinly sliced and raw elements of the classic carpaccio plate but uses Jerusalem artichoke with avocado and hazlenut instead; a rather unlikely sounding, but really delicious, combination.

Serves 4 as a starter

3 tsp lemon juice
2 tbsp extra virgin olive oil
sea salt and cracked black pepper
150g (5oz) Jerusalem artichokes
handful of watercress sprigs, to serve

FOR THE SALSA
30g (1¼oz) hazelnuts
½ ripe avocado, stone removed, peeled and flesh chopped into 7.5mm (1/3in) dice
1 generous tbsp chopped watercress or rocket leaves
3 tbsp extra virgin olive oil (or half hazelnut and half extra virgin olive oil)
1 tbsp lemon juice
salt and freshly ground black pepper

Preheat the oven to 200°C (400°F), Gas mark 6. Place the hazelnuts on a tray and roast in the oven for 4–5 minutes until the nuts under the skin are golden. Put into a tea towel, rub the skins to loosen, then pick out the nuts.

Put the lemon juice, olive oil, salt and pepper in a bowl. Using a vegetable peeler (or a mandoline), peel the artichokes, then use the peeler or mandoline to cut them into thin slices. Immediately place in the bowl with the lemon juice and oil to stop them going brown, then leave for 10–30 minutes – the artichoke will soften slightly.

Meanwhile, make the salsa. Carefully mix all the ingredients together, then season to taste.

When ready to serve, drain and dry the artichoke slices. Arrange on plates and drizzle generously with salsa, then arrange a few watercress sprigs around. Serve.

IRISH CREAM LIQUEUR
BAKED CHEESECAKE

This recipe is about as retro as it gets. In the 1970s and 80s it was hard to find a café or deli that didn't have a gelatine-set cheesecake on offer. Add a generous splash of Irish cream liqueur such as Baileys or Coole Swan and you have the quintessential Irish dessert. This cheesecake, however, instead of being set with gelatine, is baked, American-style, to give you a delicious coffee-flavoured custard sitting over a buttery chocolate base. Divine.

Serves 8

FOR THE BASE
300g (11oz) dark chocolate digestive
   biscuits
50g (2oz) unsalted butter, melted
2 tbsp double or regular cream

FOR THE TOP
500g (1lb 2oz) full fat cream cheese
150g (5oz) caster sugar
4 eggs
100ml (3½fl oz) strong coffee
100ml (3½fl oz) Irish cream liqueur

Preheat the oven to 170°C (325°F), Gas mark 3.

Put the base of a round 25.5cm (10in) spring-form cake tin upside down into the tin and secure the clasp.

Put the biscuits in the bowl of a food processor (or in a plastic bag) and whiz (or bash with a rolling pin) until they reach the consistency of coarse breadcrumbs. Tip out into a bowl, add the melted butter and cream and stir to combine. Press firmly into the bottom of the tin to create an even layer and flatten the top. Place on a baking tray, just in case any mixture leaks onto the floor of the oven while the cheesecake is cooking.

Put the cream cheese, sugar and eggs in a large bowl and whisk well to combine and to get rid of any lumps in the cream cheese. Mix in the coffee and liqueur and pour into the tin on the tray.

Place the tray in the oven and cook for 35 minutes or until almost set. There should still be a thick wobble when you give the cheesecake a little shake. Turn off the oven but leave the cheesecake inside to sit for 30 minutes, then remove and leave to cool in the tin.

To remove the cheesecake from the tin, run a small sharp knife around the side of the cake, carefully unclip the tin and, with the help of a palette knife, slide the cheesecake off the base onto a serving plate (it should slide off easily because you have turned the base upside down).

Cut into slices to serve.

GENERAL INDEX

RECIPE INDEX

PICTURE CREDITS

Photographs © Maja Smend except for:

© Catherine Crowley p93 bottom; © Chris Hill Photographic 2010 p209, p235, p119, p120-121, p190; © Fáilte Ireland p16, p37, p68 top, p69, p75, p91, p123 top left, p123 top right, p123 bottom left, p139, p141 bottom right, p143 left, p168 left, p189 , p233, p236 top, p261, p262, p281, p283; © John Mullins p40 top left , p40 bottom; © Raymond Fogarty www.aircamireland.ie p97, p118 bottom, p236 bottom left; © Rob Partis p11, p71 top left, p71 top right, p72, p90 top, p93 top left, p93 top right, p123 bottom right, p138 top, p141 top left, p141 top right, p141 bottom left, p143 right, p158 top, p161, p186 top, p187, p193, p208 top, p208 centre, p211, p217, p221, p232 top, p236 bottom right, p241, p258 top, p259, p278 bottom, p279; © Shutterstock.com p71 bottom; © Tourism Ireland p14, p36 bottom, p39 top right, p39 bottom left, p40 top right, p94, p159, p168 right, p213

Maps on p8 bottom, p36 top, p68 bottom, p90 bottom, p118 top, p138 bottom, p158 bottom, p186 bottom, p208 bottom, p232 bottom, p258 bottom, p278 top taken from Bartholomew's Pocket Atlas of Ireland, 1887 © Collins Bartholomew Ltd.

ACKNOWLEDGEMENTS

As always, there are teams of people involved in getting a book to print. I feel very fortunate to have worked with so many brilliant people on this project.

Thank you Zac Darling for working right next to me on everything I do with such aplomb. Needless to say, I couldn't do without your help and support.

This book, like all my others, goes with a television series on the same theme. All the recipes from the series *Coastal Cooking* are here on these pages. I spent a couple of months testing recipes at home with my wonderful cousin-in-law, Ivan Whelan, who was then (thankfully!) mad enough to come along for the road trip to film the series. Thank you Ivy.

Georgina Mackenzie, thank you so much for so graciously putting up with my rants, my panics, my texts, calls and emails; all in a day's work for a project editor. You deserve a medal.

James Empringham and Martin Topping, you've both outdone yourself again with the wonderful art direction. Thank you, thank you.

A big, heartfelt thanks (and baby boy congratulations!) to Natalie Jerome who really got behind the *Coast* idea right from the start and to Grace Cheetham who took over with such aplomb.

I'm so happy with the beautiful photographs in this book; the food and the scenery all look completely gorgeous. A big hug to Maja Smend who shot all the food (and me!) around my locality, ably assisted by Sam Folan. And to Rob Partis who captured the stunning raw beauty of Ireland while we were on tour filming the series.

To fabulous food stylists Annie Rigg, who styled all the food in the studio, and to Rachel Wood who came over to Ireland to style on every beach, pier and cliff in East Cork! Thank you both.

To prop stylist Lydia Brun, next time can you please leave all the stunning props behind?! Thank you Lydia.

A big thanks to the fab Liz MacCarthy who did my hair and make-up on the shoot – in the 40 mph winds and lashing rain!

Thank you to all the great people who work on the publicity for the book: Virginia Woolstencroft, Hannah Gamon, Tony Purdue, Mary Byrne, Ann-Marie Dolan and their teams, and to editors Barbara Dixon and Helena Caldon.

To Tim and Darina Allen, Rory O'Connell and the amazing team at Ballymaloe, I love working with every one of you. Thank you all for being so fab and inspiring.

Thank you so much Fionn Davenport for the huge amount of creative help, advice and insider knowledge with navigating my route up the coast for the book.

Big hugs and thanks to Fiona Lindsay of Limelight Management and her team: Alison Lindsay, Maclean Lindsay and Roz Ellman. To Conor Pyne and Diarmaid Falvey, thank you all for (trying to) keep my life in order!

We had a great TV shoot spending a month on the road from Dungarvan to Donegal with a lot of laughs (mostly at my expense, I seem to remember!) along the way. A big thanks to David Nottage and everyone at Liverpool Street Productions, Karen Gilchrist, Emma Reynolds, Rob Partis, Matt Powell, Ed Beck, Ivan Whelan, Bertie d'Basse, Karen Bracken, Gary Masterson and Cristina Moran. Thank you also to Brian Walsh.

We filmed with the most wonderful farmers, fisherman, cooks and food producers so a huge thank you to everyone who gave us so much of their precious time to help us shoot the programme.

A big cosy hug to Lucy Downes and Paula Marron of Sphere One by Lucy Downes for all the divine wool and cashmere jumpers, hats and scarves that I wore on the shoot, and also on most days of the year!

And as always, so much love and thanks to my super-amazing family, extended family and friends for always being there.

And last, but not least, thank you to all the gorgeous people who buy my books and those who I meet along the way, be it on the street or in a supermarket, who give me great feedback and continue to support me.